Recognition in the Age of Social Media

Recognition in the Age of Social Media

Bruno Campanella

polity

Copyright © Bruno Campanella 2024

The right of Bruno Campanella to be identified as Author of this Work has been asserted in accordance with the UK Copyright, Designs and Patents Act 1988.

First published in 2024 by Polity Press

Polity Press
65 Bridge Street
Cambridge CB2 1UR, UK

Polity Press
111 River Street
Hoboken, NJ 07030, USA

All rights reserved. Except for the quotation of short passages for the purpose of criticism and review, no part of this publication may be reproduced, stored in a retrieval system or transmitted, in any form or by any means, electronic, mechanical, photocopying, recording or otherwise, without the prior permission of the publisher.

ISBN-13: 978-1-5095-4456-1
ISBN-13: 978-1-5095-4457-8(pb)

A catalogue record for this book is available from the British Library.

Library of Congress Control Number: 2023934597

Typeset in 11 on 13pt Sabon
by Fakenham Prepress Solutions, Fakenham, Norfolk NR21 8NL
Printed and bound in Great Britain by CPI Group (UK) Ltd, Croydon

The publisher has used its best endeavours to ensure that the URLs for external websites referred to in this book are correct and active at the time of going to press. However, the publisher has no responsibility for the websites and can make no guarantee that a site will remain live or that the content is or will remain appropriate.

Every effort has been made to trace all copyright holders, but if any have been overlooked the publisher will be pleased to include any necessary credits in any subsequent reprint or edition.

For further information on Polity, visit our website:
politybooks.com

Contents

Introduction	1
1 Recognition	12
2 Recognition and the Media	44
3 Regimes of Visibility on Social Media Platforms	83
4 The Demand for New Dispositions	107
Conclusion	136
Notes	151
References	154
Index	177

Introduction

Everybody wants to be recognized as a useful member of society. As human beings, we evolve our sense of self through our interactions with others. We want to share values and to be part of social groups, be visible, and to be recognized by others as worthy of respect and esteem. This is fundamental for the development of our capacity for self-realization and self-determination. Throughout history, societies have developed institutions and systems that play a role in valuing what people do, achieve or represent, such as religion, legal systems, marital contracts, or even the market. Axel Honneth describes them as institutions of recognition (Honneth, 2014).

The German sociologist does not present the media as an example of such an institution; nonetheless, it is difficult to deny their key role in struggles for social recognition in western societies, particularly from the second half of the twentieth century onwards. The works of Couldry (2010), Faimau (2013), Maia (2014), Lorenzana (2016), Nærland (2019), Edwards (2018) and Nikunen (2019) are exemplary in this discussion as they see the media as a type of institution that acts upon recognition processes necessary for the development of a more democratic and free society. Newspapers, television and social media, according to these authors, are cultural and technological institutions that interfere positively (or negatively, when failures of recognition occur) in the formation of subjectivities capable of self-realization. The media are thus depicted as having an important role in the formation of a cultural citizenship, which raises questions related to the politicization of everyday life (Stevenson, 2001, p. 5).

But do all media act in the same way in recognition processes? What about social media, in particular, which have been playing an unprecedented role in structuring the ways in which subjects relate to themselves and to others? Do the unique characteristics that differentiate social media from more traditional media interfere with the development of recognition that produces self-esteem and self-respect? In direct response to the latter question, my proposal is in the affirmative. Social media operate within basically different logics from other media, logics that instrumentalize, at the individual level, social and professional relationships, and that have the potential to amplify hierarchies between people. Naturally, as will be seen throughout this work, social media have also been successfully used to strengthen the rights and social esteem of traditionally marginalized groups. This fact can be observed in the use of these platforms in individual and collective initiatives, such as the #MeToo movement. Therefore, it is important to emphasize that this book does not aim to develop a unilateral critique of the presence of social media in people's daily lives, as Desmurget (2019) and Ormerod (2020), for example, do. My goal here

Introduction

is instead to analyse what Hepp (2009) would call the 'moulding forces' of social media and their capacity to exert a determined 'pressure' on how we communicate and value each other. Ultimately, this type of pressure is not value-free.

To develop this proposal, I will endeavour to articulate some perspectives from the political sociology of recognition with an analysis of common elements that structure social media. This approach aims to show the limits of recognition produced in the everyday socialization dynamics occurring in these datafied spaces. In other words, 'likes', comments and reposts of online practices often give the idea that social media's active users are visible to their friends and followers, and, at the same time, that what they publish is valued by them. However, I propose that this type of recognition, increasingly validated and desired today, is more easily achieved by people who develop emotional, psychological and behavioural dispositions aligned with certain neoliberal ideals. That is, the incorporation of these dispositions by some of these platforms' users makes them stand out compared to those who do not have them, weakening the notion that such platforms are social spaces that promote equality – a concept present in the ideals envisioned in the early days of the internet. Moreover, I also contend that this type of recognition connected to social media, although capable of bringing material and symbolic advantages, is a weak recognition because it does not presuppose the production of a sentiment of freedom and self-respect in subjects. It is also weak because it only serves the interests of the individual seeking recognition and not both parties involved in the process, which would include the person seeking recognition and the one providing it.

To investigate these questions and their implications, this book discusses the formation and changes in modern subjectivities, and their regimes of visibility, alongside debates about social media's materiality, especially the normative principles that permeate news feeds. The book is not specifically about any one social media platform in particular, but rather about social media platforms as a whole. Although it sometimes discusses specific characteristics of platforms such as YouTube, Facebook, Instagram and TikTok, the central arguments presented throughout the chapters relate to social media platforms in general. However, this decision entails risks. Perhaps the main risk is producing generalized analyses that fail to account for the stories, transformations and specificities of each technology. But this risk is unavoidable, since this book's guiding proposal is to reflect on modifications occurring in the very habitus of the contemporary individual who increasingly seeks to relate to others and themself through different social media platforms.[1]

To emphasize the connection between these platforms and the changes in question, I develop the concept of datafied habitus. Datafied habitus is understood here as the necessary emotional, psychological and behavioural traits that enable individuals to effectively and actively engage with data-driven social media platforms as a means of shaping their identities. The process of 'datafication' of everyday life, described by authors such as Mayer-Schönberger and Cukier (2013) and Schäfer and Van Es (2017), is an important part of this debate, as it encompasses the phenomenon currently observed of metrification and economic rationalization of sociability dynamics carried out by social media. Therefore, I discuss in detail throughout this work how the process

Introduction

of datafication impacts the development of a habitus that is essential for individuals to gain recognition and value in society.

There is already a considerable body of literature analysing the emergence of self-entrepreneurial subjectivities that actively engage in seeking greater visibility and engagement in social media. Some of these works have been written based on empirical research that offers important insights into the origins and functioning of this phenomenon (Marwick, 2013; Glatt, 2022). The theoretical effort undertaken here aims to advance this discussion, but through the concept of recognition. The adoption of the perspective of recognition as the central focus of investigation, one of the principal contributions of this work, allows for a clearer relationship between the regimes of visibility favoured by these platforms and the idea of citizenship. This discussion is important because it sheds light on profound changes occurring in the individual's forms of self-representation and sociability, changes that *individualize* the process of constructing the subject's civic worth, as will be seen later. It is also worth noting that the search for recognition on social media platforms is not exclusive to digital influencers, YouTubers or celebrities. It concerns everyone who uses these platforms and who is subject to the power that these technologies have to regulate what can be seen and how it can be valued in their timelines.

What do I mean by recognition, and why should it not be dissociated from the ideas of authority and power? As alluded to at the beginning of this introduction, individuals can only fulfil their potential if they are properly recognized as competent members of society. This is a fundamental aspect of the process of identity formation, and it can only be achieved when subjects encounter others with complementary goals to their own. In Hegel's terms, recognition 'is being with oneself in the other' (Honneth, 2014, p. 44). Recognition theory is often discussed as a framework for understanding the role of conflicts in processes of social transformation. For Honneth, experiences of misrecognition and disrespect are central drivers of social movements. These movements are often characterized by a struggle to be morally and legally recognized in order to create a more just and free society. In other words, it is a struggle for normative authority (McBride, 2013, p. 6).

This book contributes to the ongoing discussion by examining how the power of social media platforms, as well as their underlying economic drivers, interferes in the processes of identity formation. Instead of investigating social struggles in the internet era, the upcoming chapters explore the context in which individual practices aimed at gaining social validation and approval are increasingly based on regimes of visibility driven by datafied logics. It is thus argued that these practices serve users' individualistic interests more than they produce transformations towards a more inclusive society. In this sense, the book proposes that these logics, often overlooked in discussions related to recognition theory, must be examined if we want to better grasp the impact of such platforms on contemporary identity creation processes.

The singularity of social media

Unlike traditional mass media, social media have a 'many to many' architecture informed by machine

Introduction

learning technologies that curate how content is distributed. They create a distinct news feed for each user, at every moment of the day, which means that they are not tailored to a specific audience formed by a group of people. News feeds follow rules dictated by algorithms that are barely understood by users but are imagined by everyone. Moreover, social media content is potentially produced by all users, making these platforms the epitome of self-representation. They also foster the false impression of being free, democratic and open. However, they are not free, because users give away personal data on their habits, tastes, connections and emotions to the platforms in exchange for their use. Social media are not democratic either, in the sense that some people have more voice than others when using them, which means that their publications reach more users. This happens not because they say more interesting, truthful or empathetic things, but because their posts better adhere to the regimes of visibility favoured by the platform. Finally, social media are not open, because they operate under opaque and constantly changing architectures.

Social media can be very personal as they frequently deal with everyday life. They work as a channel for talking to friends, exchanging cookery recipes, publishing photos of parties, holidays, etc. At the same time, social media are about getting a constant stream of feedback from friends and followers. Everything one publishes on Instagram, Facebook, YouTube or TikTok is up for judgement and evaluation. The popularity of social plug-ins, such as the 'like' or 'share' buttons, in people's daily interactions is a testament to the contemporary common desire for social recognition on media. These platforms use psychological and feedback mechanisms that encourage the formation of new connections and engagements, thus interfering with the very weaving of the social fabric (Christl and Spiekermann, 2016, p. 61). Putting these elements together, it becomes clear that social media produce a type of recognition different from that produced by traditional media.

The book's structure

This book is divided into four chapters, together with the introduction and conclusion. Chapter 1, which follows this introduction, aims to contextualize my initial interest in the book's theme and present the concept of recognition. The chapter's purpose is not to systematize debates about the concept, since this has already been extensively debated by political sociology researchers (Mattos, 2006; McBride, 2013, for example) and in other fields of social sciences. Instead, the aim is to present authors and discussions that can contribute more directly to the type of reflection that this book proposes to develop. In this sense, Honneth's (1995) three dimensions of recognition – affection, esteem and rights – help delineate the spheres in which recognition is struggled for so that individuals and social groups can fully realize their identities. This discussion is complemented by establishing some of the conditions under which the recognition process is incomplete or non-existent. The chapter also introduces Souza's (2003) articulation between recognition and the concept of habitus, which is essential in structuring the book's argument.

Chapter 2 brings media to the centre of the discussion. It provides a brief overview of studies that investigate recognition processes in media environments, with a

Introduction

particular focus on social media platforms. It argues that the analysis of recognition in such datafied spaces should not lose sight of their operational logics, which are responsible for the organization of media practices centred on creating economic value for the companies. This is followed by an examination of the news feed as a type of social space specific to social media, where these logics are manifested in the platforms' decisions about what and when to show (and hide from) their users. Ultimately, the processes of recognition on social media cannot be dissociated from a type of power unique to datafied platforms that directly interferes with how individuals and social groups are valued in society.

Chapter 3 reflects on long-term transformations in regimes of visibility in the West and how these changes influence the forms (and formulae) adopted by contemporary individuals who seek positive recognition on social media. In order to establish the basis for this discussion, the chapter introduces works on conduct and behaviour manuals written since the early sixteenth century, together with courses and tutorials aimed at people who want to increase their recognition on digital platforms. It is argued that the challenges faced today by people seeking visibility and recognition on social media reiterate the dilemmas that constitute modern subjectivity, as well as introducing new elements related to datafication processes and the deepening of economic relations in social dynamics. In this context, the chapter proposes that visibility regimes in the era of social media invest in the objectification of the self and the instrumentalization of feelings so that individuals are recognized in the spheres of affect and esteem.

The next chapter continues this discussion by examining the behavioural dispositions that constitute the so-called datafied habitus. While chapter 3 emphasizes the formation of affective regimes of visibility in the era of social media, chapter 4 highlights recent transformations in the socioeconomic context for the formation of the datafied habitus. In this section of the book, I delve further into the dispositions required of individuals who aspire to attain full recognition of their value. The chapter aims to explore in more detail what is meant here by datafied habitus, a concept that is structured around current demands for subjects' permanent connection on social media, the acquisition of a specific regime of affects, as discussed earlier, and the incorporation of neoliberal ideals of flexibility, adaptability and self-enterprise. The acquisition of these dispositions offers an advantage to the subject seeking recognition within the parameters of social media. However, in an apparent contradiction, this incorporation is simultaneously unable to create the conditions for the subject to develop lasting feelings of self-confidence, self-respect and self-esteem.

The conclusion shows how the discussions developed throughout the book complement existing works that investigate the relationship between social media and contemporary forms of self-representation and online sociability. The chapter contends that the concept of recognition shifts the focus of this relationship to the transformations in the idea of civic value brought about by the new behavioural, psychological and emotional dispositions required of social media users. In other words, the increasing importance of these dispositions strengthens the myth that obtaining visibility, followers, 'likes', etc. on these platforms is capable of transforming the individual into a citizen fully inserted into society. Finally, the chapter also raises the hypothesis,

Introduction

although not developed, that the sociocultural context of social media users interferes with the development and incorporation of this datafied habitus.

In short, recognition is crucial at both individual and social levels, but it often involves conflict. Throughout history, struggles for recognition have played a vital role in social transformation processes, enabling minority and marginalized groups to gain access to civil, political, social and cultural rights. These struggles have to do with changes in the perception and valuation of the other and, at the same time, with the collapse of the hierarchization of social relations. The act of recognizing someone activates ideals of collectivism, social justice and individual freedom.

Social media platforms promise to facilitate self-representation and a new form of collectivity by tapping into these ideals. Nevertheless, it is argued throughout this book that the type of socialization favoured by these platforms is more individual, self-interested, and, at the same time, less political. The mission of this work is, therefore, to expand the debate on the nature of recognition processes occurring on social media by closely examining how these technologies are structured and operate.

1
Recognition

Why analyse recognition and the media? The idea of exploring the concept of recognition in the context of media practices came to me a few years ago, when I was doing research on celebrity culture. I was particularly interested in the emergence of exchanges between celebrities and their followers on digital media platforms, like Twitter and Instagram. During that investigation, it was possible to observe that some celebrities who were active on social media engaged in a kind of 'economy of intimacy and recognition' as part of a strategy to motivate their fans to take part in campaigns designed to produce media attention for their idols (Campanella et al., 2018). These celebrities took part in performative demonstrations of affection towards their followers in exchange for their involvement in initiatives such as concerted campaigns with Twitter hashtags, crusades to increase YouTube channel subscriptions and even phone calls to local radio stations to request their treasured artist's songs.

Recognition

For Baym (2018), the emergence of this type of practice is testament to the mounting pressure on creators and celebrities to perform *relational labour*. Practices involving Brazilian funk singer Valesca Popozuda are a good example. During the research I could observe how dedicated she was to replying to fans' Twitter messages, phoning her most dedicated followers on special occasions – like birthdays – and even taking part in daytrips and barbecues with those who could prove to be most effective in helping her increase her popularity. On one occasion she invited fans to take part in a promotional campaign in which they were asked to post videos and photos of themselves singing her newly released single *Beijinho no Ombro* on social media. Those getting the most reactions to their posts earned the privilege of spending an entire day with Valesca.

During the investigation fans made clear that the opportunity to establish some kind of direct contact with a 'media person' (in this case, Valesca), whether in the form of a mere tweet reply, or a physical encounter, such as a 'meet & greet' session, was regarded as very special. One fan declared that Valesca made him feel important every time the two of them interacted. He felt recognized as a person of worth when she responded to his tweets or mentioned him by name. In short, these practices were perceived as a boost to his self-esteem.

In many situations, fans invest considerable emotional, time and financial resources in order to get some kind of recognition from their favourite media personality. Far from mere eccentricity, this type of sentiment just shows how media (or media people, in these cases) play such a distinctive role in the personal experiences encountered in the contemporary world (Couldry, 2012).

Recognition in the Age of Social Media

There are, of course, a myriad of reasons behind people's interest in celebrities, as the already relatively established celebrity studies field has demonstrated over the last few decades (see, for example, Braudy, 1986; King, 1987; Gamson, 1994; Marshall, 1997; Dyer, 1998; Rojek, 2001; Driessens, 2013). However, regardless of the individual drives leading to someone's engagement in celebrity-related practices, the established belief in an almost naturalized value placed on having one's existence recognized by a celebrity (or by the media) has always intrigued me. The processes responsible for the formation of this moral order are, nonetheless, rather complex. They have broader implications that clearly transcend celebrity culture. These transformations, explored in more detail in the next chapter, are the result of rearrangements in the production of modern subjectivities, connected to the growing role played by media in people's lives. The phenomenon acquired new hues in the last decade with the expansion of digital media platforms into virtually all aspects of people's daily life.

As an individual who is not very active in socializing on social media platforms, I experience a certain fear of missing out on new possibilities for establishing social connections. Nowadays, people are expected to communicate aspects of their private and professional lives as well as their stances on a myriad of issues using social media platforms. Public and private spheres are collapsing into a digital social sphere. Those who don't do it do not enjoy the array of communicative possibilities made available by digital platforms with the purpose of increasing the production of datafied sociality. The recent coronavirus pandemic exacerbated this trend even more as the need for social distancing created an extra incentive for individuals to replace

Recognition

traditional forms of social activity with online ones. There is good evidence, though, that this type of *datafied habitus* connected to our growing inclination for adopting social media platforms in our everyday socialization is here to stay.[2] By datafied habitus, I mean the emotional, psychological and behavioural dispositions needed to perform adequately and actively on data-driven social media platforms as part of the process of identity formation (more on that later). What is truly unique in this novel arrangement is that it represents a moral model that demands the subject's ability to create a type of social media existence which, in turn, becomes a product to be consumed. The near omnipresence of smartphones, personal digital assistants and digital wearable devices like Fitbits in people's lives is testament to how our intersubjective relations are being transformed towards a datafied society, i.e. a society in which social relations and daily activities are translated into data, analysed as such, and then monetized. As a consequence, I propose here that processes of intersubjective recognition are also being transformed in their different dimensions.

Before delving into these discussions, however, it is vital to delineate some of the principles connected to recognition theory in an attempt to make sense of the interrelationships between social media, subjectivity and power. The objective is not to provide a comprehensive account of the historical developments of the concept of recognition as this book does not intend to offer a critical reading of such debates. Ultimately, recognition theory is seen here as a toolbox that can help us understand how processes of identity formation and social validation are increasingly connected to the neoliberal logics informing social media platforms.

Recognition in the Age of Social Media

What do I mean by recognition?

The act of recognizing someone can acquire distinct meanings. The *Oxford English Dictionary*, for instance, divides the verb 'to recognize' into two different groupings: one connected to the operation of identifying or determining; the second linked to the action of acknowledging the existence of someone or something, to give validity. In our discussion here we are interested in the second meaning, as it relates to the idea of giving or denying value to a person or a group of people. Yet, the definition provided by the *Oxford Dictionary* is still insufficient for us, as it does not elaborate on what or who can be recognized. Moreover, it also does not sufficiently differentiate the terms acknowledging, accepting and recognizing.

In order to present a clear grasp of what exactly Honneth and other academics convey by the concept of recognition, Ikäheimo and Laitinen (2007) offer a more nuanced distinction between these meanings. They suggest a classificatory differentiation between three interconnected terminologies: identification, acknowledgement and recognition.

Ikäheimo and Laitinen (2007) propose that identification applies not only to persons, but actually to anything. Identification can be *numerical*, of a particular thing; *qualitative*, displaying singular features; and *generic*, allotting to a specific group(s). As a particular subcategory, the identification of a person or group of people can be divided into external identification and self-identification. The former involves a move where a second person identifies someone, while the latter entails a self-identification made by the person themself – although, to different degrees, self-identification is always influenced by others (ibid., p. 35). For example, the 'face recognition' feature adopted by some smartphones is, in fact, an identification system to verify that the person trying to use the device being held is the real owner of it. The technology uses facial biometrics to detect and locate specific features on someone's face in order to do that.

Acknowledgement, on the other hand, has a meaning that connects to the recognition of normative 'entities' like rules, codes, norms, principles, etc. Someone can acknowledge, for example, that a particular pledge is fair. This is to say that the entities that are acknowledged can be valued as good, authentic, genuine and so forth. Ikäheimo and Laitinen also propose that the recognition of an individual or group of people might be denied if their personhood is not acknowledged. In other words, the authors say that the acknowledgement of a person's moral status is a precondition for their being recognized. Noble (2009) extends this discussion when he argues that a politics of acknowledgement should be less concerned with questions of identity and more with a kind of ethnography of the encounter. He stresses that the act of acknowledging is not to be confined by strict boundaries, like race and gender, as it should capture the social action of the encounter of individuals with its temporal and spatial dimensions. Noble wants to draw attention to the importance of context and history in the 'countless acts of recognition' in everyday life (ibid., p. 879).

So, we arrive at our third concept, recognition. If anything can be identified, and normative entities can be acknowledged, it seems to be more appropriate to apply the notion of recognition when talking about individuals or groups of individuals. The concept of interpersonal recognition, especially in its dialogical form, is the fulcrum informing the established tradition of recognition theory. By dialogical recognition I mean that the attitudes of both, the person who recognizes and the one recognized, are necessary in the constitution of the process as a whole.

Hegel is one of the first authors, and possibly the most influential, to advance this discussion in his effort to conceptualize the stages in the development of an ethical society. The German philosopher was concerned with the processes of alienation encountered by the early nineteenth-century Enlightened individual, who was starting to experience modern ideas connected to individual rights and autonomy. If, on the one hand, these subjects had been promised individual freedom in the wake of a new ethos of modernity, on the other, they were facing feelings of society fragmentation, conflict and isolation, resulting from a decline in traditional beliefs. In his Jena Lectures, on the Philosophy of Spirit, Hegel aims to address this conflict by integrating the individual in what he regards as the modes of the spirit, viz., religion, art and philosophy. He is interested in understanding how normative expectations of personal environment are key in the formation of the subject. Ifergan (2014, p. 158) argues that this is especially true in the second part of the Philosophy of Spirit lectures, where Hegel puts the individual and the new rights-based culture of the Enlightenment at the centre of his project, while considering the traditional Aristotelian depiction of human life as an early stage of social progress.

This proposal implies a different approach to classical perspectives related to the social contract. In Machiavelli (1988), for example, the individual is in permanent distrust of the other. The sentiments of fear and lack of trust are the source of a belief that the social field is permeated by a permanent battle for self-preservation. He describes a world in which individuals and communities are in continuous competition over interests. Ultimately, humans are portrayed as self-centred beings who care only for their own good. Thomas Hobbes, who further develops this enquiry into the basis of civil life, also sees human relations as filled with suspicion. According to his theory of the State (Hobbes, 1991), this feeling of constant fear leads to the submission of all individuals to a sovereign power, in the form of the social contract.

In Hegel's perspective, on the other hand, the modern subject should not be understood in terms of competition or suspicion, but rather in their need for mutual recognition. For him, the struggle of the individual is not a form of atomistic competition but, instead, a reaction to normative expectations, which are connected to how subjects imagine they are seen by society. According to Ifergan's account of Hegel's ideas,

> Consciousness achieves existence that is first and foremost for itself when it gains the ability to recognize itself in another consciousness; self-knowledge through another consciousness provides consciousness with the means for knowing itself. This is the starting point for Hegel's discussion of the struggle for mutual recognition. (2014, p. 145)

The role played by *the other* in the formation of one's subjectivity is seen as crucial for the formation of an ethical community. This proposal forms the basis of Hegel's theory of the objective Spirit, which Honneth describes as a tripartite philosophical system. In his explanation of Hegel's proposal, Spirit is described as a succession of 'its inner constitution as such, then ... its externalization in the objectivity of nature, and finally ... its return into the sphere of its own subjectivity', also known as self-restoration (Honneth, 1995, p. 32).

In this sense, the individual can only attain self-consciousness and achieve subjective freedom if they are recognized by others. In Hegel's words, to recognize 'is to be with oneself in the other' (Honneth, 2014, p. 44). Relations of mutual recognition are a precondition for self-realization. The nineteenth-century German philosopher sees the process of recognition as a way to increase the subject's self-consciousness. According to this perspective, once I am recognized by some other, I get closer to this other and, at the same time, I gain greater awareness about the characteristics and peculiarities of my own identity, which, in turn, also demand recognition. For Hegel, social conflicts are driven by a struggle for recognition. He proposes that this process occurs within three practical dimensions: love, legal relations and solidarity. Each of these dimensions is in turn related to a different institution: marriage, Estate and civil society, respectively.

Dimensions of recognition

Axel Honneth advances Hegel's proposal by deepening the practical dimensions of recognition. Honneth suggests, for example, that not only love but also friendship and family relationships are fundamental to the formation of a basic self-confidence of the subject. These 'primary relationships' are characterized by emotional bonds shared among a relatively small number of individuals, and are fundamental to the development of the subject from early childhood. In this sense, Honneth sees in Winnicott a counterpoint to the Freudian structural model of the ego and the id, according to which the psychological evolution of the child results from monological relations between their libidinal drives and their ego-capacity. In Winnicott's account, the process of socialization with the other, especially with the mother, is fundamental in this dynamic. Childhood is the period when the first perceptions of seeing oneself in another are developed through the relationship between mother and child. In fact, the different stages of the development of a psychologically healthy child are due to changes in the structure of their reciprocal systems of interaction with the mother and others with whom they have primary relationships (Honneth, 1995, p. 99). That is, intersubjective relations are crucial to the formation of individual identity. Even in adulthood, the subject needs to be assured that they are loved by family and friends so that they have the *self-confidence* necessary to play a productive role in society (ibid., p. 104). Strong emotional bonds developed through adulthood make possible the establishment of an affectional relationship, which resembles the emotional state experienced between child and mother. By including friendship in the dimension of love, Honneth avoids confining to the sphere of family the sole responsibility for the development of a kind of relaxed form of relationship (Mattos, 2006, p. 23). Family love and friendship, nevertheless, represent a special type of recognition in the sense that they do not oblige the individual to reflect upon current norms of social regulation.

Recognition in the Age of Social Media

The dimension of legal relations also connects to the dynamic of reciprocity that pervades the dimension of love, but, differently from the latter, it was constituted during a slow and often painful historical evolution. Only with the arrival of modernity and its universal conception of the individual was it possible to conceive of the idea of an equality of rights. Honour and family status lost their centrality as the moral drivers organizing society. As Berger (1983) and Elias (2000) argue, the decline of the code of honour, which embodies a hierarchical view of society, took centuries and went through several stages. From the medieval tradition of chivalry, passing through the subsequent embourgeoisement of values which still retained some aspects of honour – especially in established groups of the elite like the military, nobility and professions such as medicine and law – the process of civilization eventually debunked old norms and roles that presupposed unequal basic human rights. George Mead, a key reference in Honneth's work, proposes that the idea of dignity gradually replaced the moral code of honour as a basis for recognition. After all, everyone can have dignity, while only a few may have honour.

These transformations addressed the problem of developing a type of recognition not founded on sentiments of personal affection but which nevertheless demanded individual attitudes empathetic towards the community. Honneth (1995, p. 115) uses the legal studies separation of individual rights in his elaboration. The first category, the negative rights, refers to the prerogatives securing individual freedom, private property and the regulation of the Estate activity, preventing it from unauthorized interference. The second category refers to the positive rights, i.e. the rights regulated by the Estate with the objective of guaranteeing the chance of participating in decisions of public interest. Finally, the third category also alludes to positive rights but, in this case, refers to the active status of a legal person which assures a just division in the supply of basic goods.

The development of these rights can be better understood in the classic study on citizenship and social class by T. H. Marshall (1950). Marshall proposes a model of gradual expansion of modern law aimed at amplifying the person's legal recognition in their civil, political and social spheres. This three-part division describes historical transformations starting in the eighteenth century and advancing well into the twentieth with the consequence of establishing new categories of basic rights. The changes delineated by Marshall were the result of demands for more inclusive forms of participation in the political community, which included not only an expansion in the types of rights being granted but also a push for universalizing the group who could enjoy them. Each new advance towards the formation of this modern model of citizenship was driven by forces 'from below' who struggled to advance the notion that every individual must be given equal opportunities to engage in the process of democratic deliberation. The introduction of the idea of equality into modern law progressed in tandem with the understanding that individuals need access to educational and cultural training as well as economic security. These principles form the basis of social rights and the welfare state, and are vital for the establishment of a sentiment of *self-respect*. Honneth argues that only when the individual recognizes themself in another do they realize that this other person has the same rights and duties as they do. In short, the legal dimension of recognition is necessary for the self-respect of the individual, which allows their participation in public life. According to Honneth, when the subject is recognized as possessing rights capable of placing them on an equal footing with others, they can fully exercise the capacities that constitute their personality.

The third and last dimension of recognition explored by Honneth is related to the idea of social esteem. Unlike the relationship of self-respect developed from the principle of universal equality between subjects, *self-esteem* involves the perception that each individual has a unique individuality in relation to others. That is, characteristics that differentiate one person from another are to be culturally valued within society. But esteem recognition can only be achieved in a group where all members of that group enjoy equal rights. Once there is legal parity among subjects, individuals entertain the possibility of feeling valued for their subjective characteristics, forming a post-traditional community. In this regard, McBride affirms that whilst legal rights should be demanded, social esteem must be earned (McBride, 2013, p. 45). This third dimension of recognition is oriented around a biographically individuated subject (Honneth, 1995, p. 127). Individual achievements are valued over social position as in the traditional honour-based society. If the latter is characterized by the long-term monopolization of opportunities for social prestige, modern society is the result of a 'collective attempt to establish new value-principles' not connected to legal privileges (ibid., p. 125). Therefore, self-realization becomes dependent on the broadening of societal value-ideas.

Recognition

What counts in the community as a valued ability and accomplishment becomes an arena of struggle. The very definitions of achievement are key for the measure of esteem that can be granted to individuals. As a consequence, culture becomes the new battlefield for struggles for recognition. The symbolic representation of individuals and groups, their singularities, values and lifestyles, must be affirmed and appreciated in the larger society. In this perspective, the necessary conditions for the development of self-esteem are part of the cultural struggles that aim to produce recognition of previously disregarded sections of the community. In this context, Pakulski (1997) affirms that the concept of citizenship, as proposed by T. H. Marshall, was expanded in the second half of the twentieth century to include a cultural dimension with the already existing civil, political and social ones. Claims concerning the singularity and importance for minority groups like indigenous peoples or LGBTQs of expressing their individuality are crucial for the extension of this type of recognition. Such groups want to enjoy legal equality and, at the same time, present their languages, identities and lifestyles in a positive perspective in the media and other symbolic spheres (Pakulski, 1997, p. 81).

According to Honneth (1995, p. 128), esteem recognition is characterized by relationships founded on a principle of symmetry that promotes the individualization and autonomy of subjects, who perceive themselves as similar to each other, while maintaining an interest in the particularities of others. Such relationships can trigger a sentiment of solidarity, which occurs when each member of society knows they are esteemed by all others to the same degree, even if they treasure different types of personal achievements and ways of life.

As noted earlier, the three dimensions of recognition conceived by Honneth describe different aspects that interfere in the formation of more egalitarian relationships between individuals. Such dynamics depend on *institutions of recognition*, understood by the sociologist as daily social practices that integrate the intentions of the subjects, producing 'reciprocal comprehensibility' (Honneth, 2014, p. 45). Love, for example, is described as a social institution of this kind insofar as it creates a mutual dependency that enables individuals to realize their reflexive aims beyond the mere desire for pleasure. Honneth additionally reminds us that Hegel expands his theory of recognition beyond intimate relations by incorporating the market as an institution that also allows the fulfilment of complementary intentions among subjects. For Hegel, the economic self-interest of individuals can be guaranteed in the market once they recognize each other reciprocally. According to this perspective, market mutual dependency is seen as engendering subject freedom. This account is, however, later problematized by Marx's description of the capitalist market as fomenting a mode of socialization not driven by cooperation, but instead by the '"alien mediator" of money' (ibid., p. 51).

Regardless of these contrasting perspectives, Honneth reminds us that both Hegel and Marx agree that individual freedom can only be achieved when subjects share their aspirations with other members of society. For Hegel, in particular, this type of sharing occurs through social practices that regulate intimate forms of relationship, exchanges that cross the market economy, as well as in different modes of deliberation in the public sphere.

Recognition

Conditions for recognition

Heikki Ikäheimo (2015) offers insightful ways to think about Honneth's theory in his analysis of the necessary conditions for intersubjective recognition to occur. The Finnish researcher proposes a different form of examining the dimensions of recognition investigated by Honneth. According to Ikäheimo, recognition can occur vertically, when it involves dynamics between persons and institutions or norms, or horizontally, when it involves only individuals. In his perspective, vertical recognition is connected to the legal dimension, as it refers to the subject's relationship with impersonal and socially accepted norms governing society. Horizontal recognition, on the other hand, can occur in a purely intersubjective form or in a normatively mediated fashion, i.e. through institutional rights or institutionalized norms. Purely intersubjective recognition, of interest in this discussion, can be divided into forms similar to those described by Honneth. In this way, genuine feelings of love, esteem and even respect result from purely intersubjective recognition inasmuch as they are not produced by instrumental valuing. Ikäheimo (2015, p. 8) argues that only an *allocentric* (in contrast to egocentric) or a *genuinely personifying* mode of recognition sees the recognizee as an individual in the strong sense of the term, i.e. as an irreplaceable other person. That is, the subject's recognition can only happen genuinely if the concern with the values and well-being of the other exists for the other, and not as a result of the self-interest of the one who recognizes them. The unconditionality of the recognition process allows the other to be seen as capable of contributing to something that I value, thus producing social esteem.

Conditional recognition, on the other hand, occurs when a person shows solidarity with another to the extent that this sentiment serves the first person's own interest and well-being. Chouliaraki (2013) offers a good example of this in her work on celebrity activism. She is interested in understanding the moral transformations underlying the participation of film stars in mass campaigns meant to generate solidarity with distant sufferers, like the victims of earthquakes or war refugees in developing countries. Her analysis of Angelina Jolie's case is emblematic in this respect. Supported by empirical research, Chouliaraki observes that Jolie's humanitarian activism is based on a self-reflective structure aimed at transforming the film star by allowing her to get in touch with her own emotions, thus resulting in a process of 'inner growth' (ibid., p. 97). Such humanitarian campaigns should hence be understood not as a form of ethicalization of the persona via the identification with a universal condition of suffering, but rather as a utilitarian strategy of self-transformation.

To complicate things further, it is also possible to argue, as I have done elsewhere (Campanella, 2020), that celebrity activism can also accrue economic benefits for the celebrities due to the qualitative transformation of their visibility. Supporting humanitarian campaigns, for example, may help to widen and qualify their media exposure, hence resulting in the production of *solidarity capital*, which can be translated into more product endorsements and other professional opportunities.

The performed demonstrations of affection by celebrities described at the beginning of this chapter can also be connected to processes of conditional recognition. The stars' efforts to engage their fans in media crusades designed to generate visibility for the idols themselves are a clear form of instrumentalization of the other in the form of esteem recognition. But this is an egocentric mode of recognition in the sense that the celebrity is not necessarily interested in esteeming fans because of their value, or in 'being themselves in this other', but rather because of the self-benefits accruing from this action.

The discussion above shows how problematic celebrity-related practices are when it comes to genuinely personifying modes of recognition. More than just people whose private lives attract public interest, celebrities are individuals whose personas are intrinsically connected to market forces in the media industry (Marshall, 1997; Turner, 2004, 2010). Celebrities' performed actions and values cannot be detached from the economic interests around which their career revolves. They depend on the production of 'accumulated media visibility through recurrent media representations' in order to sustain their special capital and status (Driessens, 2013, p. 553). In the age of social media, this means that they need as many followers and reactions to their online profiles as possible if they want to stay visible. This necessity, however, compromises the unconditionality of the relations they establish with followers and fans, mainly because those are self-interested relations. In other words, social relations developed by celebrities with their fans are frequently colonized by market principles, which limits the possibility of them engaging in unconditional forms of recognition.

It is worth observing though that celebrities and digital influencers are only the more successful personifications of an increasingly common model of individual that uses self-representation strategies on social media in order to gain media visibility and, whenever possible, transform this visibility into symbolic or material gains (Marwick, 2013; Senft, 2013; Khamis et al., 2017; Duffy and Pooley, 2019).

It seems clear, therefore, that the greater presence of media-related logics in the individual's social life makes the processes of purely intersubjective recognition more complex than what is traditionally described in sociology. As the next section proposes, this growing media presence is also connected to new models of subjectivity permeated by practices that occur in digital communication platforms. This is to say that media platforms not only communicate different identity references, something explored by researchers linked to cultural studies for many years (for example, Kellner, 1995), but they are also increasingly perceived as producing the space where subjects want recognition processes to take place.

Recognition and identity

The works of Charles Taylor on multiculturalism, identity and recognition are some of the most influential references in the field. Alongside Honneth's *The Struggle for Recognition*, Taylor's 'Politics of recognition' (in Taylor, 1994) sparked the debates in the early 1990s around Hegel's development of this concept.[3] But, while Honneth's work is mainly based on Hegel's early Jena Lectures (Hegel, 1983), Taylor founds his discussions on the later *The Phenomenology of Spirit* (Hegel, 1977). In 'Politics of recognition' Taylor advocates the encouragement of cultural multiplicity, the stimulation of particular languages and not discriminating against different sexual orientations. This is a departure from traditional class struggle debates, which marked most of the twentieth century, towards a focus on identity and culture as a fighting field to combat oppression (McBride, 2013, p. 9).

Taylor's championing of *identity politics* is grounded on the idea that each person bears their own originality, which should always be respected and encouraged. Individual and group singularities are, according to this account, the driving force behind how each person ought to conduct their lives. For him, this is the result of the formation of the modern subject and their structure of *self-expressiveness* (Taylor, 2001, p. 488). Following Trilling's description of the 'ideal of authenticity' (Trilling, 1972), Taylor argues that individualized identities developing from the late eighteenth century onwards are built upon the understanding that the person has to be true to their self, their own intuition and particular way of being (Taylor, 1994, p. 28). In other words, individuals should express their own measure of things, not conform to external inauthentic pressures. Fundamental in Taylor is his understanding that identity politics is to be applied to social groups as well, especially minority and disfranchised ones. Indigenous peoples, LGBTQ, ethnic and other minorities have their own values, languages and cultures, which should hence be recognized and valued by society at large.

His defence of a politics of difference and expression was a reaction to debates on higher education occurring in Canada in the last decades of the twentieth century, and can be seen as his response to 'difference-blindness' liberalism. The latter represents a politics of universal dignity which supports the idea that all humans are intrinsically equal, and should therefore be treated as such. This perspective vocalizes beliefs not aligned with policies aimed at emphasizing the singularity and cultural integrity of minorities. Even when an apparent compromise is reached through the implementation of temporary measures, the goals behind politics of difference are still distant from the politics of equal dignity. When, for instance, university quotas based on ethnicity are implemented as a provisional solution to establish a level playing field, allowing old blind rules to resume at a later moment, the wish to permanently cherish distinctness and expression is not taken into consideration. After all, politics of difference praises 'the potential for forming and defining one's own identity, as an individual, and also as a culture' (ibid., p. 42). For Taylor, this capability to be different must be respected – not just for a limited period, but forever.

Most of the criticism of his perspective on recognition centres on Taylor's defence of multiculturalism and identity politics as a field of struggle against oppression and inequality. Nancy Fraser (1995), for example, defends the idea that recognition alone is not capable of solving material inequalities in society. To deal with that, she proposes that the notion of recognition must advance conjointly with redistribution. For Fraser, claims for cultural change should be associated with demands for economic and material change as well. Moreover, such reorganization should carry a transformative character capable of restructuring the 'underlying generative framework' (ibid., p. 82). Her project aims at deconstructing cultural boundaries that, for example, invest in defining what a gay and lesbian identity may be, as well as social boundaries that set economic class divisions. In this sense, queer politics and socialism are two sides of the same transformative strategy proposed by Fraser. Social justice, she proposes, is possible when distinct types of group differentiations are blurred.

Thinking about recognition through habitus

Despite the power of arguments against the identitarian perspective of recognition defended by Taylor, it is worth taking a closer look at his work, especially his description of the emergence of the *punctual self*, which is connected to the politics of universal dignity. Most of his critics direct their assaults to his optimism on the potentialities of multiculturalism, identity politics, and the correlated ideals of authenticity and subject expressiveness. These ideals are part of what Taylor calls the *expressive self*. For the author, both models of the self, the expressive and the punctual, are the basis of a moral topology defining the modern subject.

I argue here, however, that Taylor's account of this moral model of the punctual self can be productive for making sense of the relationship between recognition and media practices in datafied environments. In fact, it can also shed a light on the issue of recognition in different socioeconomic and national contexts, an issue not explicitly addressed by either Honneth or Taylor. For this purpose, I draw particular attention to the articulation that Brazilian sociologist Jessé Souza makes of the theories of Charles Taylor and Pierre Bourdieu.

Souza (2003) attempts to develop a sociological theory capable of accounting for what he calls the 'social construction of sub-citizenship', a phenomenon he believes is found mainly in countries of the Global South, such as Brazil.[4] For him, Global South societies do not share a history marked by internal processes of western rationalization. Quite the opposite, Souza argues that these countries received a sudden influx of material and symbolic culture from western nations such as the UK, the USA and France, marked by a dynamism and vigour which left little room for any kind of concerted resistance (Souza, 2003, p. 96). This assault was directed by colonialist forces coming from the outside and destabilized existing moral norms. For this reason, Souza suggests that in Global South societies the punctual self, described by Taylor as a product of struggles for recognition linked to the universalization of dignity, never took hold in the deeper and more complete way that it did in Global North societies. In the latter, the introduction of the welfare state, for example, represented the historical consolidation of a process of pacification and social homogenization that resulted from the spreading of bourgeois ideals responsible for the formation of an emotional economy centred around self-control, self-discipline, flexibility and the valuing of reason.

Taylor draws his description of the punctual self from the work of John Locke, in particular his theory of the western modern subject. For Locke, the latter is the result of a movement of disengagement from religion and tradition, and the concomitant adoption of disciplinary practices meant to consolidate a rational control over the self (Taylor, 2001, p. 173). The Enlightened subject turns inward to become aware of their own activity. Therefore, disengagement, for Taylor, 'demands that we stop simply living in the body or within our traditions or habits, and by making them objects for us, subject them to radical scrutiny and remaking' (ibid., p. 175). The institutional anchoring of the punctual self, its methodical discipline and capacity for self-development are the building blocks of the universal dignity of the rational agent emerging around the late sixteenth to early seventeenth century. In Taylor's own words, the punctual self requires 'the ability to take an instrumental stance to one's given properties, desires, inclinations, tendencies, habits of thought and feeling, so that they can be *worked on*, doing away with some, strengthening others, until one meets the desired specifications' (ibid., pp. 159–60; italics in the original).

Far from constituting a fortunate historical coincidence, this change was actively and consciously wrought over the course of several centuries.[5] According to Souza, this slowly maturing process which created a 'social imaginary' (Taylor, 2004) never occurred in countries like Brazil where, until the late nineteenth century, the economy was based on the labour of a vast population of slaves who were never recognized as individuals worthy of freedom and dignity. In this type of society, the processes necessary for the adoption of the psychosocial requisites of the punctual self were historically absent, at least until the twentieth century. There are a few reasons for that. Some of these populations shared a colonial history of violence and exploitation, which resulted in them not having their dignity properly recognized by segments of society in power. Additionally, disciplinary institutions like hospitals, schools, workhouses, which regulated the rational subject, were not universally available. These are some of the key factors that hindered a process of disengagement and objectification of the subject which is crucial in instilling a common sense of autonomy and mutual recognition. In short, Souza argues that universalizing forms of recognition linked to the idea of a basic dignity shared by all strata of society never took root in Latin America and other parts of the Global South.

The reasons for this situation are complex, and it is beyond the scope of this book to probe into them. Evidently, the consolidation of a moral model of the punctual self in developed western societies does not mean that disputes surrounding it have disappeared. In fact, they have surged in the last decades, among other reasons as a result of the decline of the welfare state, the precarization of labour relations and the increase of migration flows to Global North countries. These unsettling developments not only have resulted in more inequality but, what is more important for the argument of this book, have coupled with the expansion of datafied capitalism to modify the dispositions necessary for subjects to be recognized as individuals of equivalent worth, as will be examined further ahead.

Despite this, Souza considers that the ideal of the punctual self is still markedly more consolidated in western nations. Along similar lines, Taylor also proposes that conflicts surrounding recognition in European and North American countries take place mostly within the field of culture, linguistics and community, favouring a politics of difference mainly linked to ethnic minorities, feminist and LGBTQ groups and the politics of multiculturalism (Taylor, 1994, p. 25). These struggles occur within a framework that places value on difference, a characteristic of the expressive self.

Souza draws on Pierre Bourdieu to articulate the different models of the self described by Taylor within the context of the Global South and the idea of sub-citizenship. Bourdieu is known for his decisive contribution to our understanding of the mechanisms that naturalize social difference through structuring structures that act directly on the practical experience of the subject within the cultural field (Bourdieu, 2000). Yet, according to Souza, Bourdieu did not realize the extent to which his analysis of the formation of class habitus was unable to take the different levels of moral learning, which go beyond barriers of social category of this sort, into account. In other words, Bourdieu's analyses of class formation through a system that inscribes evaluative and perceptive structures on different strata of French society are linked to the conditioning influences of lifestyles and worldviews. The bodily inscriptions of habitus, as Bourdieu describes them, operate at a cultural level, in the common understanding of the term: that is, linked to the most trivial choices of daily life including those that are connected to taste (Bourdieu, 2002). Thus, taste is not something that is inherent to the individual but a marker of class that structures social hierarchies from an early age, through the pre-reflexive and spontaneous practices inscribed on the body itself. Hairstyles, ways of speaking and dressing, eating habits, etc. are markers that all of us bear and through which economic inequality is naturalized.

Notwithstanding the forms of social stratification constructed, to a large extent, through routine practices linked to the field of culture, Souza argues that Bourdieu presumed, albeit implicitly, the existence of a moral perspective widely accepted by the French society of his day, premised on the fundamental equality of subjects. In Souza's view, this meant that in France as well as in other western societies there prevailed a basic respect for the other, regardless of social class, signifying that all were seen as '"useful" members of society, albeit unequal in other dimensions' (Souza, 2003, p. 176). This is to say that people are recognized for their claims of personhood (Ikäheimo and Laitinen, 2007). In short, Souza argues that Global North countries are characterized by a shared universal level of dignity, the fruit of a 'long march' that consolidated an equitable moral vision of the individual.

But, as happens with all analytical simplifications, things are more complicated. Initiatives in the last decade like #BlackLivesMatter and the #MeToo movement have made this type of proposition more problematic indeed. No one doubts, for example, that, even in the present day, African Americans suffer from a structural racism in the US that prevents this segment of the population from experiencing more universal forms of recognition. Needless to say, similar forms of social injustice happen with distinct social groups in the US and in other western countries as well (Kallen, 2004; Warwick-Booth, 2013). Nevertheless, it is difficult to deny that in non-western countries like Brazil, larger segments of society have historically encountered lower levels of access to civic, social and political spheres of citizenship if compared to traditional western societies.

The type of 'shared habitus' described by Souza operates at a moral level and is responsible for a fundamental equality presuming that all subjects are useful members of society. Following his argument, this habitus is deeply rooted and precedes the habitus that Bourdieu describes. For this reason, the Brazilian sociologist calls it *primary habitus*. Its configuration is connected to the moral predispositions of a social group or individual that enable them to be legally[6] and

Recognition

symbolically recognized as full-fledged citizens, able to act as a productive force in society. That is to say, this is the habitus of the punctual self, which, according to Taylor, appeared in the late sixteenth century in the wake of the emergence of bourgeois institutions responsible for ideals of self-discipline and ability to work.

In the contemporary world, however, Souza proposes that the punctual self should not be understood exclusively as a development of a moral view presuming the existence of universal dignity as a source of recognition. The productive capacity of an individual – the result of the disciplining processes analysed in depth by Foucault (1972, 1979a) and the instrumental rationality described by Weber (1958) – is a crucial element for apprehending current sources of dignity. Put differently, people are recognized today, in the universal sense of the concept, not merely because they are rational agents worthy of dignity. Instead, they are recognized as subjects insofar as they acquire the social and individual requisites that turn them into productive agents within society.

Jessé Souza does not discuss the role of media in the formation of the contemporary punctual self, yet he does signal the relevance of certain individual configurations linked to the productive field as necessary for the creation of self-confidence, self-respect and self-esteem. In Souza's view, the most basic type of recognition in today's world must be thought of in terms of Reinhard Kreckel's concept of the 'ideology of performance' (*Leistungsideologie*). Greatly summarized, Kreckel proposes that only the 'full-fledged citizen' (*Vollbürger*) can experience the kind of recognition that allows for the formation of a self-fulfilling identity (Kreckel cited in Souza, 2003, p. 168). For him, in order to acquire this condition, one must possess the three elements that together make up the 'meritocratic triad': position, salary and qualification. This triad not only serves to legitimate differential access to personal and professional chances in life, but also places the category of 'labour' in a fundamental position, enabling the subject to form their personal identity completely. The absence of minimal individual capacities for successful competition, according to Kreckel, prevents the consolidation of personal self-esteem and social recognition. The constitution of these conditions is the result of the development of that which Souza refers to as the primary habitus. In Souza's words,

> primary habitus implies a set of psychosocial predispositions reflected in the sphere of personality, the presence of the emotional economy and of cognitive preconditions for a performance suitable to attend the demands (variable in time and space) of the role of the producer. (Souza, 2011, p. 135)

The absence of these preconditions makes the comprehensive recognition of the individual difficult, at the same time as it generates the fragility of their social condition. It is for this reason that Souza denominates precarious habitus the 'lower limit' of primary habitus (Souza, 2003, p. 167). The precarious habitus is structured through behavioural, emotional, cognitive and even nervous dispositions, as Duarte's work on the 'mental' constitution of the urban working classes in Brazil similarly suggests (Duarte, 1986). This state of precarity restricts the individual's ability to hold a productive role such as that described by Kreckel.

Given the difficulty of building a more concrete distinction between the two types of habitus, we could think about it through the idea of inclusion (primary) and exclusion (precarious),[7] or even citizen and 'under-citizen'. The latter would refer to individuals who do not reflect the presence of the primary habitus. These are excluded not only because they are not fully recognized in their civil, political and social spheres but, most importantly for Souza, because they have not mastered the individual prerequisites necessary to actively accommodate themselves to contemporary economic imperatives.

Although it may be possible to argue that the reality of developing countries such as Brazil is marked by the existence of large segments of society which are economically and socially excluded, as a result of complex historical factors (Fernandes, 2008), the growing global demand for flexible, competitive subjects makes the precarious habitus increasingly evident in almost all societies. Ultimately, Souza is proposing that recent labour and social transformations, demanding not only an emotional economy and psychological inclination of a particular type but also a flexibilization of the individual, have increased the disparity between primary habitus and precarious habitus. In other words, he argues that the personal requirements necessary for the individual to be recognized in the universal sense, i.e. to be perceived by society at large as a full citizen, have become more demanding in the last decades. In this context, the Brazilian sociologist contends that there is a diminishing sense of social equality not only in Global South countries, but also elsewhere.

Souza's argument has key implications for the Taylorian project and for this book as well. One important element in Taylor's defence of multiculturalism and the politics of difference as the basis for individual self-determination is the notion that the struggle for citizen dignity and universal equality has been, in some ways, won. As discussed earlier in this chapter, Taylor advocates that the ideal of universal dignity, which replaced the moral of honour from the early seventeenth century onwards, is so well established and accepted in western countries that the struggles for recognition in the contemporary world should focus instead on self-expressiveness and the valorization of individuality. Hence, Souza's claim that the general acquisition of personal dignity is a problem not restricted to developing nations anymore, but is instead an important issue facing developed countries as well, gives a renewed impetus to the matter. In this regard, the challenges faced by the moral model of the punctual self should be seen to be as important as the ones faced by the expressive self for the development of the personal identity of the individual in all its capacities. Failing to do so would risk legitimizing a 'consensual background', to borrow from Kreckel, of the differential value of human beings, which is implicit in the ideology of performance (Kreckel cited in Souza, 2011, p. 134). Struggles for recognition in the contemporary world should thus be understood in terms of individual and social differences as well as of individual and social similarities.

Generally speaking, Souza describes a change in the individual configurations connected to the productive field occurring in the last few decades which demands a more qualified, flexible and emotionally conditioned subject. However, even in his more recent works, he does not offer any clue as to the impact of the media, and more specifically social media, on these transformations, which is understandable considering that Souza is not a media theorist. His main concern is to understand the implications of the logics of colonialism and, more recently, of capitalism, in the development of a precarious habitus, linked to a type of 'sub-citizenry'.

Some academics, however, argue that contemporary datafied society has inaugurated a new form of colonialism, *data colonialism* (Thatcher et al., 2016; Couldry and Mejias, 2019a). They warn us about the naturalization of personal data extraction by big tech corporations and the subsequent management of people through these data. Souza's discussion helps us engage in this debate, but from a particular angle. If we accept the idea that there are indeed new requirements for the primary habitus, i.e. new demands for the subject to be recognized in the most basic sense, and that these requirements are connected to the individual capacities to perform under increasingly difficult circumstances, then we should ask if and how datafied social platforms take part in these transformations. In a sense, this is the key theme that animates the main discussions ahead.

Ultimately, recognition is a concept that can help in articulating the ways in which the expansion of economic and technological logics that convert processes of socialization into data is being internalized and transformed by individuals. The social requirements necessary for constituting a person's identity in all its potential are in permanent rearrangement. The general valuation of what counts or what does not count as personal achievement, for example, has evolved over the centuries as the result of struggles by oppressed segments of society. Over the twentieth century, the field of culture became a particularly key site for battles over recognition, as was discussed earlier in this chapter.

2
Recognition and the Media

How do the media transform processes of recognition and identity production? In order to tackle this question, the present chapter develops a brief review of works investigating recognition processes in media environments, with a special focus on social media platforms. The aim is not to analyse all works on the topic; instead, the idea is to use a number of articles, chapters and books that portray recurrent perspectives on the theme, and which serve to illustrate the arguments put forward here.[8]

I wish to argue that the search for recognition on social media platforms should not be confined to the perspectives employed by research on the traditional mass media. Social media operate in the social sphere of the news feed, which has an impact on how the individual makes the world intelligible (Bucher, 2018). In this sense, platforms like Twitter, Facebook, TikTok and Instagram, responsible for a considerable portion of today's sociability, modify the very principles structuring the idea of recognition. Publishing, liking, sharing and commenting are just some examples of social media practices implicated in contemporary dynamics of recognition. What is distinctive in these new dynamics though is that they imply a type of sociability marked by a process of datafication, i.e. a process in which people's connection with others is put 'in a quantified format so it can be tabulated and analyzed' (Mayer-Schönberger and Cukier, 2013, p. 165). The process of datafication in social life predates the invention of digital technologies and is a result of the increasing use of various media in communication. This phenomenon is part of a larger trend, which is discussed in the chapter.

It is, nonetheless, crucial to observe that within processes of datafication social practices are transformed into data and are then rewarded by algorithms based on their ability to generate more data and financial gains. The news feed is especially significant in this regard, as it gives materiality to the logics behind these algorithms to platform users. This chapter argues that research on recognition in media environments, particularly social media platforms, should consider the material quality of these platforms and their working logics, which are geared towards generating economic value for companies.

Although scholars like Maia (2014) and Lorenzana (2016) have used Honneth's recognition theory to explore how social media can amplify voices that have historically been silenced, they have not examined whether these platforms operate under rationalities that challenge the very idea of recognition and its potential to produce collective solidarity and equality. The sections below suggest that analyses of recognition in these datafied spaces should consider the platforms' working logics, which dictate how economic value is created for their companies.

The chapter examines the news feed as a social space unique to social media, where the platforms' working logics are manifested in decisions about what to show or hide from users. Research on recognition in social media should consider how platforms collect and process data and how this information rewards particular forms of media practices. Ultimately, recognition processes on social media are intertwined with the unique power of datafied platforms, which affects how individuals and social groups are valued in society.

Mediated recognition

Debates on recognition theory are not new, but they gained traction in the 1990s within the fields of political sociology and philosophy.[9] Many of the works published in that period were concerned with theories on social movements, identity politics and social justice. Over the years the concept has not only proven its continuous value for addressing these issues, but it has also expanded its reach to other academic fields, such as political science (Ringmar, 2002), public health (Mendonça, 2011) and housing policy (Feldman, 2004; Sanches, 2022).

Media and communication theorists started to use recognition theory in a more or less consistent way from the early 2000s onwards. John Peters, an early enthusiast of this debate in the field, offered an elaborate defence of the importance of intersubjective recognition in communication (Peters, 1999). He draws on

Recognition and the Media

Hegel to propose that communication processes are fundamental for the establishment of conditions that allow mutual recognition. As seen in chapter 1, Hegel suggests that the subject cannot be self-sufficient or even exist without the other, or without being recognized by the other. Subjectivity is, for Hegel, a two-sided coin. Communicational processes are, therefore, critical for the subject's discovering of aspects of their interiority, which would be otherwise inaccessible. This occurs, according to Peters' account, because individuals are not fully aware of their inner selves, since they are constituted by elements which are only available to the world outside the subject. That is, the individual depends on the other to acquire self-knowledge. 'For Hegel', says Peters, 'the self has no privileged access to itself: it only finds itself *post facto* or in another self, who has recognized it as a self' (Peters, 1999, p. 277). In short, communicational processes are fundamental for the subject to be recognized and, thus, to acquire knowledge about their selves.

The works investigating the processes of recognition in media environments use different terms to refer to the phenomenon, such as 'mediated recognition' (Maia, 2014; Lorenzana, 2016; Muscat, 2019), 'mediatized recognition' (Cottle, 2007), 'cultural recognition' (Malik, 2014) or simply 'recognition' (Couldry, 2010, 2012; Mendonça, 2011; Raisborough, 2011; Faimau, 2013; Bargas and Maia, 2017; Martins and Bastos, 2017; Edwards, 2018; Nærland, 2019; Nikunen, 2019; Davies, 2021). In common, they all see the media as an institution that acts upon recognition processes necessary for the development of a more democratic and free society. Newspapers, television and social media platforms, according to their stance, can produce spaces for deliberation and social representation that interfere positively (or negatively, when failures of recognition occur) in the formation of subjectivities capable of self-realization.

In this respect, Couldry (2012) sees in Honneth (1995) the basis to reflect on the risks deriving from unequal, or even failures of, recognition of segments of society by the mainstream media. Most media cultures, suggests Couldry, produce 'the gap between representation and lived experience' (Couldry, 2012, loc. 5275). Recurrently, media coverage of minority groups is done through stereotyped presentations that increase social divisions. Failure to recognize is not simply linked to the contempt for or devaluation of another person, it is the very negation of the 'status of a full partner [of this person] in social interaction, able to interact with others as a peer' (Fraser, 2000, p. 114). Using the notion of political listening, Muscat (2019) offers a representative example in her research with news audiences in the city of Sydney, in Australia. She shows how mainstream media discourses are key in establishing racialized notions of otherness, usually through negative representations and practices of exclusion. While some participants in her research confronted mainstream mediations of racism, they contradictorily expressed Islamophobic fears, thus reflecting existing values articulated by these same media. For Muscat, the results are evidence of the key role played by public service and community media for facilitating political listening and, ultimately, processes of mediated recognition.

Malik (2014) sees similar challenges presented by media representation in her analyses of the European context. In her view, the approach of European public service broadcasters to minority groups presents two imbricated principles: 'multiculturalism on the one hand and equal citizenship on the other' (Malik, 2014, p. 38). Again, she proposes that unbiased representation in public services is a central strategy for ongoing struggles aiming at group recognition and social justice.

Ultimately, having their own voice heard and valued by society at large is central for these not fully recognized groups. In this respect, Couldry argues that the use of alternative media by indigenous peoples, inhabitants of the peripheries of large cities and other minority groups could encourage the development of an active political and civic agency. In his words, 'recognition solutions are much more likely to come via acts of media *production*'[10] (Couldry, 2012, loc. 5285). With the use of websites and local radio stations, these groups expand their voices beyond their living spaces through the sharing of memories and experiences, previously invisible to the rest of society.

The articulation between voice and recognition is made even more explicitly in another work, in which Couldry draws on Honneth (1995) to rethink the very theory of democracy (Couldry, 2010). In *Why Voice Matters*, he suggests that the individual's capacity to realize their abilities as human beings and to be widely recognized before the rest of society is connected to a more democratic way of life. Any notion of social justice must, therefore, be linked to the plurality of voices that can be heard, whether through alternative media or not. Recognition demands some freedom of action of the individuals so they can fulfil their capacities, deliberate about the organization of social life and contribute to society.

For Cottle (2007), television journalism should engage in these processes of giving voice to the voiceless and rehabilitating the representation of 'former others'. Mediatized recognition, he argues, can be achieved through deliberation and the public display of differences, which results in increased political respect for asylum seekers, refugees and other minority groups.

Taking a similar perspective, Edwards draws attention to the role to be played not only by mass media, like television and newspapers, but also by public relations. She reports the results of a study on YouthVoice, a UK charity that helps young people to speak out about issues that matter to them (Edwards, 2018). YouthVoice offers the skills and material support to marginalized individuals to open up 'localised spaces of appearance', prompting responsive listening from different segments of society. While her research demonstrates the importance of this type of initiative, it also draws attention to the tensions arising from the constant (re)framing of identities involved in the process (Edwards, 2018, p. 330).

Serelle and Sena (2019) also discuss the formation of identities in their analyses of the struggles for mediated recognition related to films and theatre plays. They investigate the backlash against two recent Brazilian productions: a play based on the true story of a transgender person who was tortured and assassinated in the mid-2000s and a film depicting the slavery period in Brazil. Both productions received severe criticism from members of social movements for perpetuating problematic race and gender representations as well as for their casting choices. While the slaves in the film *Vazante* (2017) were portrayed as passive, flat and voiceless individuals, the transgender *Gisberta*, in the play of the same name (2018), was interpreted by a cisgender actor, which was seen as an act of silencing transgender voices. Serelle and Sena argue that the complaints levelled at the productions proved that both fictional and non-fictional storytelling should pay careful attention to the demands of voice and recognition when representing underprivileged groups.

Notwithstanding the value of all these contributions, Rousiley Maia's *Recognition and the Media* (2014) stands out as a telling example of work which extensively explores the relationship between media and recognition. In the book, Maia and her collaborating researchers present Honneth's sociological programme in detail in order to lay out the theoretical foundations for her research on representation of minority and stigmatized groups in different media. The authors use a range of methodologies to investigate the various cases explored in the book. They conduct qualitative examination of media material, run 'focus groups' to develop interactive contexts and combine framing and content analysis to identify discourses on issues related to recognition. The articulation between power and the media is discussed, mainly in relation to the construction of discourses and representations of disadvantaged and minority groups in television series and newspapers articles. Hence, the power of media organizations, especially mass media, is read from their capacity to reflect and produce cultural and political meanings, a stance overtly inspired by the Frankfurt School tradition (Maia, 2014, p. 4). The authors are particularly interested in understanding how minority groups seek to exert pressure to change the production practices of media organizations in order to promote a more inclusive society. According to Maia and her collaborators, the disadvantaged groups portrayed in the cases studied do manage, on occasions, to successfully challenge the decisions related to the creation and circulation of social representations taken by traditional mass media agents.

The chapters in Maia's book investigating the struggles for recognition in the online context, however, pay little attention to the power exercised by digital platforms, such as Facebook or YouTube. The latter, for example, is basically portrayed as an infrastructure that allows various social actors to become content producers. In other words, the depiction of YouTube in the book centres on its simplicity and its potential to allow plural and conflicting views to coexist. The platform is represented as a space where free conversation and deliberation take place, even if, sometimes, in a conflictive and disrespectful fashion (Maia, 2014, p. 161). But such description leaves out a key type of governance performed by YouTube's algorithms in relation to what is published and what is made visible, which reconfigures the distribution of what can be seen, heard and thought (Rancière, 2009). YouTube's materiality is therefore treated in a soft manner. Moreover, this perspective also ignores the development of *algorithm imaginaries* (Bucher, 2017), which have a direct impact on how people feel and relate to the workings of the platforms, ultimately interfering in the building of practices connected to identity formation. In this sense, the issue of media power in Maia's case studies suddenly loses traction when it comes to analysing struggles for recognition on social media platforms. To put it differently, the structuring economic logics of these platforms which are acting on the horizon of the subjective possibilities of its users are simply ignored.

Recognition and the Media

This issue can also be perceived in the ethnography Lorenzana (2016) conducted with Filipino transnational citizens living in India. In his work, Lorenzana analyses the daily practices on Facebook employed by Filipino migrants as strategies to convey esteem and social recognition. He shows how the publication of photos and texts displaying professional achievements and affirming social connections plays a fundamental role in the identity formation of these individuals. This is particularly evident when members of the migrant community convey their skills and contributions to the Indian society on the social media platform (Lorenzana, 2016, p. 2192). Although Lorenzana acknowledges that Facebook predisposes users to self-representation, he does not advance a proposal to investigate how this occurs or the implications of this finding.

As seen in the debates above, discussions on deliberation theory and media representation are the structuring frames of debates articulating social recognition and traditional mass media, such as TV and newspapers. Nevertheless, these perspectives appear to show their limitations when it comes to analysing recognition processes on digital platforms. The works of Maia and Lorenzana, for example, share a generally positive perspective on the possibilities offered by YouTube and Facebook for individuals to express their voices. If, on the one hand, the case studies reported by the researchers successfully demonstrate how such platforms provide the space and symbolic resources for recognition to take place, on the other hand, they do not reveal what the conditions and the context are in which the production of these resources takes place. As Couldry and Mejias argue, social media companies are responsible for processing social relations following logics that, in their words, 'hollow out the social' (Couldry and Mejias, 2019b, p. 115). These companies convert sociability into metrics which are then analysed, processed and ranked in order to produce economic value.

Duffy and Pooley (2019) argue that such rationalities restrict the expressive possibilities of the subject and do not fit into individualized models of self-promotion. They shape the cultural and cognitive frames that are more valued in society. Couldry also warns that mythical accounts of new forms of political mobilization enabled by digital platforms do not consider the encouragement of 'short-term loyalties and less stability in political socialization' (Couldry, 2015, p. 608).

Social media and their earlier accounts

In the late 1990s and early 2000s, several academics, who articulated identity, digital media and 'cyberspace', reflected such mythical accounts (Rheingold, 1994; Negroponte, 1995; Turkle, 1996; Jones, 1998; Lévy, 1999a; Dodge and Kitchin, 2001). Amongst them, Henry Jenkins is certainly one of the most notorious defenders of the internet as a space where individuals can express themselves and make available their works and ideas freely, without the intermediation of traditional mass media. For him, 'grassroots movements' on the internet can use their acquired mobilization capacity to (re)negotiate power over cultural production, previously controlled by a handful of communication groups. The possibility of debating TV series on online forums and circulating videos on social networks indicates, in his view, an intrinsic potential for the sociopolitical transformation of society. 'Right now,' assures Jenkins, 'we are mostly using this collective power through our recreational life, but soon we will be deploying those skills for more "serious" purposes' (Jenkins, 2006, p. 4). The author seeks inspiration in academics such as Pierre Lévy, who praises the transformative potential of a kind of 'collective intelligence', a hallmark of virtual communities in his view. According to the French philosopher, the combination of the individual knowledges of each member of these groups can pose a threat to the hegemony of corporate capitalism. He perceives 'collective intelligence' as an achievable utopia (Lévy, 1999b).

Along similar lines, Mitra takes a sociological perspective in her contention that the internet is a space where the 'marginalized can use their new-found digital voice to utter the call for acknowledgement' (Mitra, 2001, p. 31). She praises the hyperlinked connection of voices assisting the formation of new communities where subordinate groups can challenge existing conventional narratives about them. In short, the cyberspace is, in a reference to Hall (2021) and Spivak (1988), where alliances can be made so unspeakable stories can be told, and individual agents can exercise discursive power. Mitra employs Bakhtin's concepts of discourse to argue that, on the internet, the dispossessed can overcome barriers posed by dominant groups, who traditionally controlled channels of communication to speak *about* the 'other'. Within cyberspace's open structure, proposes Mitra, marginalized groups produce their own identities and adopt an *internally persuasive discourse* to defy stereotypical identities created by *authoritative discourses* (Mitra, 2001, p. 45).

Recognition in the Age of Social Media

A more complex understanding of social media

Despite Mitra's and Jenkins' correct understanding of the profound transformations in power struggles over representation of identities brought about by the internet, they adopt a rosy perspective of cyberspace architecture that leaves out more nuanced views of the friction occurring within these spaces. This type of stand, however, has become less common over the years as emerging empirical studies began to concentrate not so much on the promises of specific network designs, or on abstract ideals of a new online agora, but on the actual social dynamics taking place online.

This is the case, for example, with Balleys et al.'s (2020) study of processes of social recognition of teenagers on YouTube. The authors combine content analyses of the videos produced by teenage creators with a reception investigation of these videos by a similar age group. Balleys et al. show that the search for social recognition implicates a common sense of intimacy. Successful young YouTube creators manage to develop a style of self-presentation that forges the idea of closeness and 'community building' practices. These YouTubers not only adopt traditional para-confessional strategies used by celebrities, like sharing intimate secrets (King, 2008), but also exchange common identity markers. The authors argue that the processes of recognition observed in the research are twofold: 'It is both a capacity to recognize oneself in others – like figures with whom one can identify with [sic] – and a need to be recognized by others, that is, to be seen as an individual with social value' (Balleys et al., 2020, p. 8). Their article demonstrates how teenagers deploy different strategies on YouTube to build a type of community of shared values that plays an important role in their identity formation. For instance, creators not only ask their audience to comment on, 'like' and share their publications, but they also mention them or even invite them to appear on their videos. They do so in order to increase the sense of authenticity of the social bonds, and to affirm identity reference models.

Both Balleys et al. (2020) and Lorenzana (2016) present research that investigates media practices on digital platforms that aim to increase the perceived social value of specific social groups. The authors show how these groups struggle to be recognized by performing in particular ways. In Lorenzana's study, for example, the Filipino transnationals living in India use Facebook and traditional media to re-examine their identities and present themselves as valued professionals against a background of negative stereotypes related to Filipino migrant workers. By doing this, they strive not only to increase their esteem but also to affirm their connections with significant others who also provide recognition. Participants in Lorenzana's research stress the importance of posting about personal and career achievements on Facebook as a strategy to gain social status.

Balleys et al. and Lorenzana touch on a key issue related to digital social platforms, namely their capacity to predispose users to self-representation in ways that positively (re)affirm their social identities. Nevertheless, it is crucial to draw attention to the fact that these and other similar works base their discussions on the analyses of particular publications, photos and videos created and watched by the platform users, which clearly foster valued personal identity models. But what I argue here is that Facebook, YouTube and other digital platforms are much more encompassing in the processes of subjectivity production than these works reveal.

Certainly, as noted above, the teenagers studied by Balleys et al. deploy different strategies on YouTube to build their community of shared values, so important to their identity formation. At the same time, the agency that YouTube exerts in these teenagers' lives surely exceeds the dynamics analysed. In fact, the research in question does not show which other types of YouTube videos this audience watches, how they reach these videos, and in what ways YouTube recommendation systems and algorithms interfere in this circuit. Moreover, although the authors recognize the existence of financial incentives structured in the platform for creators to adopt an intimate confessional style (ibid., p. 9), they do not discuss the implications of that.

Needless to say, answering all these broad questions is not the objective of Balleys et al., nor ought it to be, as they represent a different research agenda. The point here, which will be explored in more detail in the next chapters of the book, is to argue that digital social platforms like YouTube play a larger part in processes of social and individual recognition than is usually acknowledged. Over a decade ago, Gillespie (2010) already drew attention to the fact that YouTube is much more than a platform for individual expression, merely a channel for publishing videos with specific content. The author examines the intricate relationship between platforms and governance, and discusses how platforms, as private entities, are increasingly entangled in public policy debates and regulatory discussions. Ultimately, he showed how the term 'platform' was employed by YouTube in ways that mask the lack of neutrality by the company as a content deliverer while, at the same time, emphasizing its capacity to foster users' creativity by offering a 'raised, level surface' (Gillespie, 2010, p. 358).

In this respect, Bishop (2018) argues that YouTube's algorithm privileges and rewards specific classed and gendered content connected to consumerism. In addition, she also proposes that, according to the case studies investigated, YouTube creators have particular understandings of the workings and logics of the platform's algorithm, which are then assimilated in their forms of self-branding and other related practices.

Similarly, it is difficult to measure the importance of Facebook when it comes to the development of individual self-confidence and self-esteem. To be recognized is to be seen as a useful member of society. There are several forms frequently deemed capable of producing and signalling someone's value on Facebook. They are usually associated with the number and the importance of friends and followers someone has on the platform, and the significance of the reactions to that person's publications, which can contribute to a sentiment of social validation. These forms constitute the basic analytical framework used in research studies dealing with mediated recognition like, for instance, Maia (2014), Lorenzana (2016) and Balleys et al. (2020). The problem is that this framework does not take into consideration how digital platforms collect, treat, hierarchize and monetize all the bits of information that organize these forms of recognition. After all, this organization is key to the production of the social structures we inhabit (Couldry and Hepp, 2017). If the power associated with traditional media lies, in part, in their concentrated capacity for creating a particular symbolic meta-capital (Couldry, 2003a), the power of digital platforms sits astride its capacity to determine, following its own economic interests, the content someone will be exposed to (Van Dijck et al., 2018).

Digital platforms act directly on what Rancière calls the 'distribution of the sensible' and on the configurations of the experience. What can be seen and when something can be seen on Facebook depend on decisions taken by the platform algorithm based on how it perceives each one of its users and their online relations. For Rancière (2009), the individual, as a citizen, should take part in the governance of their own life in order to be properly recognized. But that demands access to what the author denominates 'a common', which can be thought of as a distribution of space, time and activities connected to the possibility of participation. The French philosopher argues that there is no distinction between the sphere of politics, the sphere of speech and the social. Thus, the political action does not occur only in the classic sense of the term. It happens, fundamentally, in its capacity to exercise governance over the sensible: that is, over what can be seen, heard, said and thought. He talks about a politics of aesthetics, but not as a discussion of art theory. Instead, he is interested in a regime of identification and thought, in a mode of articulation between manners of making, forms of visibility of these manners and modes of thought (Rancière, 2009, p. 17).

In this respect, the questions that should be asked when investigating struggles for recognition on digital platforms must go beyond the discussion of who has the power to produce representation or who has access to the creation of media meta-capital, to also ask how the sensible is distributed, by what logics, and with what consequences.

The problem now faced by such enquiries is that, unlike in the era of mass media, there is a growing interdependence of everyday life and data-driven systems. According to Couldry and Hepp, '"data" and "information" generated by systems of computers are today a precondition for everyday life', their processing '[is] consequential for social life' (Couldry and Hepp, 2017, p. 123). And the results of this data processing that criss-crosses most aspects of the subject's routine are the production of social knowledge itself. Couldry and Hepp remind us that the traditional theory of the social construction of reality developed by Berger and Luckmann (1966) assumes that common-sense knowledge could be created by the combination of parallel perspectives on how knowledge comes to light in people's everyday 'social contexts'. However, Couldry and Hepp suggest that this is more problematic now as the role played by data in people's lives is more unintelligible in specific social contexts.

It is not only that individuals and social groups have to learn new competences in order to give visibility to their value and self-realizations in a datafied society, but also that the very definition of what counts as self-realization and how to achieve it changes. One could argue that the conditions necessary for recognition to take place depend, to a certain extent, on the construction of social life by systems based on algorithms. To advance this argument I propose here that nowhere can this be better observed than in the news feeds of social media platforms.

The news feed is a space *curated* by social media platforms, which aim to give access to a personalized construction of social life. In Facebook's terms, this space shows stories and news that *'matter most'* to people. The platform defines it as 'a personalised, ever-changing collection of photos, videos, links and updates from the friends, family, businesses and news sources that you've connected to on Facebook'.[11] How a news feed curates, personalizes, and how it defines what matters most to its users is of huge importance and, at the same time, a relatively opaque issue. Taina Bucher rightly proposes that the news feed 'is political insofar as it is exercising a position of governance' (Bucher, 2018, p. 67). It relates to the 'different ways of being in the world'. In a nutshell, news feeds construct regimes of visibility as much as regimes of invisibility, which have huge influence on the construction of social life.

The next sections of this chapter will explore how the transformations brought about by media in general, and more recently by data-driven platforms, have changed the very nature of social relations. According to Couldry and Hepp (2017), the wave of datafication is the fourth and most recent stage of a long process of mediatization to take place in western society. For them, digitalization and datafication are 'associated with a much more intense embedding of media in social processes than ever before' (Couldry and Hepp, 2017, p. 34). News feeds will be analysed, in this respect, as a concrete space of encounter where the social meets the 'techno-commercial strategies' employed by digital platforms (Van Dijck et al., 2018, p. 33).

Datafication of social life

The datafication of social life should be understood as a process that started long before the creation of digital technologies. It is part of a larger phenomenon related to the growing presence of different media in communicative instances. Krotz (2007) proposes the term *mediatization* as a concept capable of accounting for a development not confined to a particular geography or culture. Mediatization is one of several meta-processes outlined by him as 'constructs which describe and explain theoretically specific economic, social and cultural dimensions and levels of the actual change' (Krotz, 2007, p. 257). Along with globalization, individualization and commercialization, mediatization cannot be studied empirically. It can instead be thought of as a working idea used for understanding the impact of the expansion of distinct forms of communication in our daily life. The study of mediatization is associated to a medium theory connected to the traditions developed by scholars like Innis (1951), McLuhan (1967), Meyrowitz (1985) and, more recently, Peters (1999, 2015), which relate the changes in materiality of media to historic transformations of society and culture.

Hjarvard (2008, 2014) takes an institutional approach when discussing the phenomenon of mediatization. He equates the media to politics, family and education as institutions capable of (re)producing specific relations between individuals, according to certain normative orientations. Social systems, in this perspective, are influenced by and become dependent on the media logic. For Hjarvard (2014, p. 202), this institutional approach has a few advantages. It captures long-term structural changes between the media and different social spheres; allows the study of media-related social and cultural affairs at the meso-level, thus avoiding too general or too detailed analyses of social interactions; and permits the capturing of the interdependency between media, culture and society. The author uses structuring theory to argue that mediated communications provoke institutional transformations. In other words, mediatization produces an overlap between media and other institutions such as politics and religion, which internalize some of the logics associated with the media. Hjarvard (2014, p. 216) argues that this happens because the media provide a public sphere where society can reflect on its important matters, concerning all institutions. He also notes that institutions are gradually going through a process of virtualization as a consequence of the growing presence of different media in people's daily life. Smartphones, for example, are rapidly disembedding social practices from the physical world, something that became even more accentuated during the COVID-19 pandemic. Lastly, Hjarvard proposes that the media have also become a quasi-independent institution with its own affordances and characteristics, which are exported to other institutions.

Livingstone (2019), nonetheless, takes a more reticent approach to the matter. She contends that perspectives like the one defended by Hjarvard put too much weight on the media logics and their influence over institutions. She advocates a dialectic view that pays more attention to media practices of the audience rather than to a takeover by the media (Livingstone, 2019, p. 175). Livingstone is correct in her preoccupation that a mediatization theory that basically examines the functioning of power 'from above' runs the risk of silencing the lived experience of the audience.

Hepp (2009) also problematizes positions that assume a homogeneous and linear media logic. He instead advocates the investigation of the mediatization of specific cultural fields. In this sense, mediatization is seen as a process with qualitative aspects as well as quantitative. By a quantitative view of mediatization he means a position that takes into consideration the increased number and types of media technologies available. Simply put, people can now access these media from almost everywhere, all the time, and in very distinct social contexts. From a qualitative perspective, the process of mediatization mobilizes the 'moulding forces' of the media, which exert a determined 'pressure' on how we communicate (Hepp, 2009, p. 143). Following this logic, smartphones can be seen as devices that not only allow but actually exert some pressure on people to stay permanently connected. Print, on the other hand, deploys a different moulding force. It permits the development of more profound argumentations, compared, for instance, to television, because it facilitates the structuring of complex ideas. Hepp crucially stresses that, despite the specific affordances of each medium (Gibson, 1979), nothing is a given in relation to their effect upon culture and society.

In a more recent take on the matter, Couldry and Hepp (2017) suggest that a 'figurational approach', as originally proposed by Elias (1978), is, perhaps, more productive for understanding the interweaving process between the media affordances, on the one hand, and individual agency, on the other. They propose the analysis of the relations between the actors, their orientations, and the objects and technologies used in these relations. Ultimately, Couldry and Hepp (2017, p. 67) want to examine the stabilization of patterns of associations between these dimensions in order to unmask the power relations producing social meanings. Figurations can involve, for example, discussion threads on Facebook and their interconnected ecology of content circulation that may include strategies of self-promotion, friendship development, etc. This proposal allows for a better comprehension of the new 'datafied social order which relies more on infrastructural force (or near-force) than on the openly contestable legitimacy of norms' (ibid., p. 212).

In fact, the question of social order and its formation is key for debates on mediatization. It has been, for example, at the heart of Couldry's investigation on media power and ritualization. In this sense, one can argue that the issue of mediatization was present in his research before he formally used the concept. His longstanding interest in Catherine Bell's take on ritualization, defined as a process which allows 'the objectification of oppositions and the deployment of schemes that effectively reproduce the divisions of the social order' (Bell, 1992 cited in Couldry, 2003b, p. 30), reflects his preoccupation with understanding the role of media in the (re)production of social categories. This concern applies to both more traditional mass media and newer data-driven platforms.

Couldry's early reflections on mediatized forms of experiencing everyday life sit along an axis that connects theories informed by perspectives on rituals and ritualization (Turner, 1974; Douglas, 1984; Durkheim, 1995; Bell, 2009) with works that explore forms of naturalization and legitimation of power (Barthes, 1973; Foucault, 1988; Bourdieu, 1990). Media ritualizations, following his account, are processes in which society '"takes cognizance of itself" (Turner, 1974, p. 239), or rather *appears* to do so' (Couldry, 2002, p. 285). The latter part of this quote is key to understanding his central concern about the implications of the burgeoning role of the media in 'framing' the individual's experience of the world. This approach devotes particular attention to the institutional mechanisms (of the media industry) of the representation of the social, implicit in his *'appears to do so'*. In other words, Couldry is concerned with the creation of an invisible and pervasive power, structured on a media meta-capital (Couldry, 2003a), which affects the 'exchange rate' between the symbolic capital in different social fields.

This insightful investigation of the relationship between social order and the media was mainly focused on traditional media like television, newspapers and radio. When I was studying fan practices in Brazil some years ago (Campanella, 2014), it was possible to see how digital media platforms like Twitter were used in new forms of ritualization, which, in some respects, are not so different to those analysed by Couldry. Some fans, for example, organized syndicated publications of specific hashtags at a particular time of the day in order to simulate a type of 'live event' capable of producing more traction and visibility in the platform's trending topics. This kind of practice, which took advantage of Twitter's 'trending topic' feature, formed part of the fans' efforts to increase the visibility of their beloved celebrities. One of the striking aspects of such practices is that they were particularly common when fans wanted to draw attention to the imminent participation of their idols in a television talk show or radio interview. In other words, the fans studied often decided to simultaneously publish some pre-established content on digital platforms in order to draw attention to an impending traditional media broadcast involving a celebrity. In a sense, these fans were using digital platforms to draw attention to the idea of 'liveness', which is one of the 'thought categories' linked to the idea of the *mediated centre* developed by Couldry (2005) – by which he refers to the myth that there is a centre of society to which the media have special access.

When elaborating the concept of media ritual, Couldry stipulated a few categories (or 'thought categories') that work in the naturalization of this special status claimed by media companies as representatives of the social. The first and most important classification level is the one differentiating what is '*in* or *on* or associated *with* "the media" and anything that is not' (Couldry, 2005, p. 65; italics in the original). Similarly to the differentiation made by Durkheim (1995) between the profane and the sacred, the categories of media ritual encompass the social world completely, and although it is a constructed idea, it eventually becomes natural through its repeated use. Celebrities, for example, are individuals who belong, by definition, to the media world, which automatically gives them a special status. The next level of classification is directly connected to the previous one, and deals with the notion of hierarchy within the media. The concept of 'liveness', for example, reinforces the belief that what is presented by the media is more relevant than what is not, due to a (supposedly) greater connection with reality. Any live broadcast should, according to this proposition, represent a more accurate perspective of the world if compared to a recorded event that has already taken place, even in the recent past. In this sense, the fan practices described above are a type of media ritualization which legitimizes the power of traditional media, especially because of their reliance on different layers of the idea of liveness.

Although the idea of the mediated centre is still useful, for example in some studies of media practices involving popular YouTube videos, I follow Couldry and Mejias (2019b) in recognizing that there are new, powerful forces working in the organization of the social that do not rely on the traditional forms of media ritualization. The huge capacity of datafied platforms for collecting and processing data gives them an unprecedented ability to frame social life. In this sense, Bell's concern with the reproduction of the divisions of the social order can be transposed, contemporarily, to a preoccupation with how people connect with others and with the world. Corporations responsible for creating digital platforms are changing the very nature of the patterns of interactions (figurations) in social life. According to Couldry and Hepp (2017, p. 53), this reflects a deepening of the mediatization process as the technology-based interdependence intensifies. They talk about mediatization as a process that comes in waves, the first being mechanization, marked by the invention of the printing press, followed by electrification, which is connected to the telegraph and the telephone, and, more recently, the wave of digitalization, usually related to the computer and the internet. For Couldry and Hepp, data-driven technologies, such as the social media platforms discussed here, inaugurate the next wave of mediatization: *deep mediatization*. They demarcate an era of datafication, in which not only the production of knowledge but also, and perhaps more troublingly, the constitution of the self is transforming at an unprecedented pace.

The role of the news feed

Andersen (2018, p. 1147) proposes that deep mediatization 'implies a different form of human interaction and cognition than any previous set of media has demanded from or forced upon us'. The actions of searching, ordering and archiving are routinely enacted as part of the process of making the world intelligible. Search engines and algorithms are, in this respect, crucial for the production of the contemporary social world.

Nowhere has this been better observed than in the now infamous Facebook/Cornell 'emotional contagion' project (Kramer et al., 2014). This was a massive-scale experiment in which almost 700,000 users of the social media platform were exposed to emotional expressions on their news feeds. The objective of the experiment was to discover whether people would change their posting behaviour when in contact with different emotions. The investigation was heavily criticized when its results were published, drawing condemnation of both Facebook and Cornell University for not seeking explicit consent from the participants. The latter were not aware that they were taking part in an experiment, which aimed at secretly manipulating their behaviour. Although much of the outcry regarding the test arose from its appalling lack of ethical principles (Puschmann and Bozdag, 2014; Schroeder, 2014; Meikle, 2016), it is important here not to lose sight of its findings.

To be precise, Kramer et al. conducted two parallel investigations with distinct groups of people. In the first one, they reduced the exposure to negative emotional content on the users' news feed, whilst in the second group, they did the opposite, i.e. reduced the positive emotional material. The authors concluded that both investigations indicated a clear emotional contagion. A decrease in the expression of positive emotions in a person's news feed, for example, made that person publish less content with a positive emotional disposition, and vice versa. In this respect, the news feed can have a buffer effect in the creation of particular types of emotion of Facebook users. The experiment also demonstrated that less exposure to either form of emotion in the news feed resulted in less expressiveness and engagement, of any nature, of that person on the platform in the following days (Kramer et al., 2014, p. 8790).

The results of this experiment are testament to the power of the digital social platforms. It is a power connected to the capacity for categorizing the world, but also the power to build, for example, different emotional dispositions in the social world. Facebook can directly interfere in how the reality is presented to its users, not only in the form, but also in the content, in order to provoke specific responses from them. Hence, it is patent that this capacity also interferes in the production of visibility and recognition of individuals using this technology.

It is also crucial here to draw attention to the fact that the experiment took place specifically in the news feeds of the participants. This means that all the content that was deliberately omitted in their news feeds never became unavailable in the profiles of the people who produced it. This means that if a particular participant in the experiment visited the profile of their Facebook friends, he or she could always see everything that was posted by them. This is evidence of the role played by the news feed as the main space for intervention of the platform. It is there, in the news feed, where Facebook puts its effort into curating the stories and news that, in its words, 'matter most to people', but ultimately also matter most to Facebook.

Bucher argues that we must consider the algorithm systems behind the news feed as political devices as they reflect particular views on 'how the world is to be ordered' (Bucher, 2018, p. 67). For Facebook, as with other social media platforms, it is crucial that the news feed works to validate a form of 'participatory subjectivity that hinges on continued and ongoing engagement with the platform' (ibid., p. 155).

If, on the one hand, the democratization symbolized by free and easy access to Facebook's news feed makes it possible for the expression of social esteem and recognition of the diverse voices that make up society, on the other it also restricts and conditions intersubjective relationships within dynamics that privilege practices closely linked to capitalist logics (Fisher, 2009). To help in understanding how social media platforms articulate processes of datafied recognition, I propose to reflect on the way they translate and operationalize what Honneth calls *expressive gestures of recognition*, that is, the demonstration of 'emotional readiness to morally engage with the addressee' (Honneth and Margalit, 2001, p. 122). Although Honneth and Margalit refer to smiles, respectful greetings or nods when exemplifying these expressive gestures in the face-to-face world, we can imagine that the act of liking or sharing content on social media platforms can also be seen as a type of expressive gesture of recognition.

For Bucher (2018), Facebook and other social media news feeds pose novel challenges for the contemporary subject. Such technologies do not follow the traditional panopticon architecture described by Foucault (1979a). Bentham's panopticon described by the French philosopher is based on a regime of equal distribution of visibility in which every individual is submitted to the same degree of potential examination by the disciplinary power. Power is exerted by the *possibility* of the subject being visible all the time. A schoolboy, a worker or a prison inmate is never certain whether they are being watched, leaving an uncertainty that makes them adjust their behaviour to the governing norms. The principle behind the architecture of the news feed, nevertheless, is quite different. People actively want to be visible to them. As Bucher argues, 'in Facebook, there is not so much a "threat of visibility" as there is a "threat of invisibility" that seems to govern the action of the subjects' (Bucher, 2018, p. 84).

Honneth and Margalit (2001) suggest that a person has to be visible in order to be recognized. In fact, and this is also key here, visibility in the literal sense is also a prerequisite for invisibility in the figurative sense (Honneth and Margalit, 2001, p. 114). This means that for a person or a social group to experience a lack of recognition, which is similar to being figuratively invisible, they have, prior to anything, to be physically visible. Honneth and Margalit remind us, for instance, that the nobility was traditionally allowed to be naked in front of personal servants because the latter were figuratively invisible, despite their physical presence. The servants were there, but not recognized as worthy individuals capable of provoking discomfort or shyness in the noble. Their lower status as persons precluded their capacity to affect individuals of a higher rank.

The first chapter of this book explored how minority groups and excluded segments of western society struggled in the last couple of centuries to be legally and symbolically recognized as worthy citizens. In fact, one could argue that this is a permanent quest driving the actions of common individuals who want to see their personal and professional achievements valued by society. This is no different in the age of social media platforms' ubiquity. What is peculiar in the present context, however, is that frequently individuals are only certain that they are figuratively visible, i.e. that they are valued by others, when they see some kind of positive response from friends or followers on social media, even when these responses are simple expressive gestures of recognition, or, as Plessner termed, 'allegories of a moral action' (Plessner, 1970 cited in Honneth and Margalit, 2001, p. 118). People want to be visible online through their publications, reactions and updates, but they wish to do so in such a way that their followers respond accordingly via, for example, comments, shares or 'likes'. In short, social media platform users want to be visible in both senses, literally and figuratively.

But, in order to do so, they have to accept and internalize some broader economic principles informing social media platforms. Facebook, Instagram, Twitter and so on are structured in such a way that they can collect and process as many data as possible from their users in order to create economic value for the companies. Not only must people agree to have their own personal data gathered and shared by the platforms but they have to fit their sociability into a language that serves capitalist ideals. In this sense, it is impossible to separate the working dynamics connected to the creation of visibility and recognition on social digital platforms from the production of data and financial profit.

Therefore, it is suggested here that expressive gestures of recognition taking place on social media platforms are structured within a framework of actions that advances the economic interests of tech companies, which eventually hinders the core principles underlying

Recognition and the Media

traditional struggles for recognition. As seen in the last chapter, Honneth and Taylor propose that the action of recognizing the other reinforces the notion of equality between people and, at the same time, affirms the singularities and differences among individuals and social groups. However, the process of being recognized in datafied environments is, sometimes, at odds with moral perceptions that see individuals as having a common and universal dignity and, at the same time, restricts expressive possibilities not committed to logics that transform the subject into a commodity of themself.

In short, this chapter argues that most works dealing with mediated recognition focus their perspectives on the struggles for positive representation of groups and individuals on different media. Discussions involving mass media, like TV and radio, have traditionally concentrated on representation and on disputes over practices of media production. Similarly, the more recent works on recognition in social media often echo debates on the potentialities of what is frequently portrayed as a kind of new public sphere. Such works emphasize the symbolic resources provided by platforms such as Facebook, Instagram and TikTok. In this view, social media are mostly characterized by the possibilities they open up for the expression of voices from both shared individuals and historically marginalized groups.

What is missing in this story, however, is a more detailed discussion of some typical features shared by these social media and their implications for the processes of social and individual recognition. Their news feeds, in particular, should be analysed as an especially important type of social sphere where processes of capturing, translating, valuing and rewarding are being performed by technologies and systems that yearn to make people stay connected for longer periods of time while, at the same time, predicting their actions and consumer choices.

The quantification of the social

Considering the importance of social media and their news feeds for contemporary processes of recognition, I propose here a more detailed discussion of some typical features shared by these platforms. It is clear that TikTok, Facebook, Instagram, Twitter and YouTube have specificities that differentiate one platform from the other. Nevertheless, they all share some common governing principles that underline this discussion on datafied recognition. These technologies are heavily dependent on a curatorship carried out by their algorithms to decide what and when to show to their users. The news feeds are particularly important in this task. It is in the social space of the news feeds that the processes of capturing, translating, valuing and rewarding the publications become concrete to the users of these platforms. This is the basis of such technologies and systems as strive, as argued above, to make people stay connected for longer periods of time.

The conversion of human sociability into metrics is at the core of datafied platforms. This is a process by which people's connection with others is organized in such a way that it can be rearranged, classified and scrutinized. In other words, datafication has to do with reorganization.

In 2007, Gary Wolf and Kevin Kelly, both editors of *Wired* magazine, initiated the Quantified Self

Movement,[12] a project that preaches 'self-knowledge through numbers'. The initiative aims to bring together researchers, programmers and others interested in developing new quantitative methods of individual self-knowledge. For participants of the community, what cannot be numerically measured cannot be improved. In this sense, Wolf and Kelly propose that measuring physical activities, functional rates of the human body, food consumption and even people's social life is fundamental for self-improvement. Far from being an eccentricity, this initiative reflects a broader movement observed in the present time: the metrification of everyday life.

The use of metrics in society is, nonetheless, not new. Hacking (1990, p. vii) reminds us that the increasing use of statistics, tables and averages in the nineteenth century unleashed new forms of social engineering that gave substance to what was conventionally called the 'normal person'. The objective, according to Hacking (1990), was to intervene in the behaviour of the 'undesirable classes'. Crime and suicide rates in cities were used as parameters for public security policies and for the management of specific social groups. But, according to Ajana (2018), the phenomenon has reached new heights in recent decades. As the Quantified Self Movement proposes, the wide use of quantitative evaluations is no longer restricted to government, institutional and business spheres, but becomes part of the everyday life of the common subject. The author indicates that the development of digital technologies has made possible the widespread adoption of self-tracking devices, such as Fitbits and Apple Watches, as well as social media platforms that use metric principles to assess the most diverse everyday social practices.

What is most striking in the phenomenon, however, is not simply the enormous volume of data produced today, but, as Ajana (2018) points out, the rationalities and discourses created from them – just as was the case, for example, in Hacking's (1990) study of the objectification of knowledge in the nineteenth century, where he shows that the use of numbers has historically served as a tool for government and control of populations and individuals.

In the present context, there is a clear expansion of this type of logic which quantifies the individual's actions and social dynamics, within a scenario where identities are increasingly valued from numerical perspectives. This phenomenon is especially evident on social media platforms. Regardless of the particularities of each of them, these dispositives[13] convert intersubjective dynamics of recognition among their users into numbers and scores. The introduction of the 'like' button by Facebook in 2010, for example, paved the way for the conversion of sociability into metrics, which not only optimize the monetization of individual scores and data produced across platforms, but also facilitate strategies for creating engagement. Gerlitz and Helmond (2013) state that both the 'like' button and other social plug-ins are potential triggers for numerous processes aimed at producing more online participation. According to the authors, people engage more with content on platforms that demonstrate a greater number of 'likes' and shares, a process that clearly favours a feedback logic.

Bucher (2018, pp. 77–8) also argues that the more reactions a Facebook post generates, the more 'edges' are assigned to it by the platform. An edge is a type of attribute which was originally composed of three

Recognition and the Media

dimensions, each with its own score: the type of interaction (comments, shares, 'likes', etc. have different weights); the temporality of the interaction (more recent interactions usually have greater weight); and who was responsible for carrying it out (greater affinity between a user and a follower or friend on the network results in more weight). To estimate the relevance of an object within Facebook – which can be a published image, a post, a video, an external link, etc. – the algorithm multiplies the values of each edge it generates to create a final score, which is then used to decide the hierarchical position of this object in the news feed of each relevant user. The weights of these valuations, as well as decisions about the ranking of objects, are dynamic elements defined by artificial intelligence systems that seek permanent optimization capable of generating more engagement and time spent by users on the platforms.

This model, described in detail a few years ago by Sanghvi and Steinberg – engineers responsible for developing Facebook's news feed – has already undergone numerous modifications and has become more complex, as demonstrated by De Vito (2016) in his analysis of the patents approved by the platform over the years. The very concept of EdgeRank, used by Facebook in the early 2010s, fell into disuse after a short time. However, even though the ranking of different types of publication in the timeline has incorporated other dimensions, such as prior engagement, platform priority, content quality, capacity for creating more interactions, among many others, one essential characteristic seems to remain stable over the years: a constant creation and redefinition of different affinity rating scales between users and objects on Facebook. More recently,[14] the platform published an updated technical explanation of its news feed algorithms, which also mentions the use of information regarding past engagement of its users as well as diversity rules aimed at offering a mix of types of content. Facebook uses literally thousands of *signals*, a term more in vogue nowadays, to evaluate what a person might find more relevant in their news feed.

These signals and affinity scores are the backbone of social media platforms' algorithmic systems. Bucher (2018, p. 11) argues that Facebook's evaluation of online friendships, based on different affinity criteria, 'serves an essential role in sustaining the social networking system itself'. Ultimately, the higher the affinity score within a friendship on the platform, the greater the chance that Facebook will use that relationship in promoting its products. For the author, 'friendships [from the perspective of these technologies] are nothing more than an equation geared toward maximizing engagement with the platform' (Bucher, 2018, p. 11).

The measurement of friendships on Facebook and other social media platforms, however, goes beyond the computational systematization of connections. It is a vital part of the visual experience of its users, which, as Grosser (2014) points out, influences their evaluation of what is read, seen and watched. Thus, the visualization of the number of 'likes' or shares received by an object directly influences a user's decision to react to that same object. In other words, the more eloquent the numbers of engagement or expressive gestures of recognition a publication receives, the more it will be perceived as relevant by users. As a consequence, this type of logic puts pressure on users to get more reactions to their publications.

Recognition and the Media

There are a number of studies suggesting the negative effects on mental health caused by 'compare and despair' attitudes on social media (Hampton et al., 2015; Royal Society for Public Health, 2017).[15] But even these disturbing effects offer economic opportunities for entrepreneurs who create 'digital detox' programmes that help deal with issues related to continuous digital engagement (Kuntsman and Miyake, 2019). Amidst this debate, Instagram proposed in 2019 to 'depressurize' the experience of using the platform by hiding 'like' counts from its news feeds in some regions of the world. To justify the decision, Vishal Shah, Instagram's Head of Product, affirmed that 'the act of expression itself is what we cared about, not the validation, or perceived validation, that a public like count gets people'.[16] However, after observing that overall engagement in the platform declined as the result of the removal of this feature, a consequence also detected in a study by HypeAuditor,[17] Instagram decided in 2021 to offer the choice to show again the 'like' counts of users in all regions where it had been made unavailable. So, despite the pressure experienced by its users when comparing the metrics of engagement on the platform, and associating it to their own personal value, Instagram decided that it was more important to reintroduce the 'like' count, i.e. their tool that makes visible a quantitative measurement of the success of posts.

It is worth noting that while digital platforms facilitate the establishment of intersubjective connections in many and diverse ways and transform them into metrics, they simultaneously monitor and watch over such connections, even if this occurs in imperceptible ways by users. Exchanging 'likes', making comments, posting and watching photos and videos online are actions that result in a huge amount of data that is processed in order to transform users' intersubjective relationships into products (Couldry and Mejias, 2019b), which is another consequence of the expansion of this culture of metrics.

3
Regimes of Visibility on Social Media Platforms

What are the regimes of visibility in the age of social media, and why it is important to understand them when researching recognition? It is proposed here that the desire to be seen and recognized as a worthy subject through practices in social media cannot be divorced from the emergence of specific regimes of emotion, affection and self-regulation. If, on the one hand, these regimes in western countries date back to long social and psychological transformations experienced over the centuries, as described by Elias (2000) and Wouters (2007), they are also the product, more recently, of new power relations linked to the datafication of social life. This chapter seeks to explore some ideas about the transformations in these regimes, examining, among others, Elias's reading of the work *De Civilitate Morum Puerilium*, by Erasmus of Rotterdam, the online course for digital influencers offered by Brazilian YouTuber Whindersson Nunes (Nunes, 2018) and recent research by Araújo (2021) on 'algorithmic norms'.

Facebook, YouTube, Twitter and other social media platforms are important spaces for deliberation and social representation, as argued by Maia (2014), Lorenzana (2016) and Balleys et al. (2020). These technologies can help connect plural voices and assist the formation of new communities, where subordinate groups can challenge existing conventional narratives about them. But the ability of such platforms to establish new regimes of visibility also gives them an unprecedented capacity for framing social life. Corporations responsible for creating these technologies are changing the very nature of the patterns of interactions (figurations) in social life (Couldry and Hepp, 2017).

Hearn, for instance, draws attention to the emergence of new forms of validation of the self being created in datafied environments. This is the case with the account verification system launched by Twitter, later introduced by other social media platforms as well. Twitter users with verified accounts are not only given priority in the platform's news feeds, but also more credibility. According to Hearn, the symbolic capital conferred by Twitter through account verification 'legitimates attention-getting forms of self-presentation as the means to achieve social recognition and, potentially, profit' (Hearn, 2017, p. 69). It should not be forgotten, however, that the platforms are the sole arbiter of this process. They have the unique power to define and assign such recognition through opaque criteria that are largely based on metrics that measure the reputation and influence of users.[18] In this sense, the verification of accounts can be read as part of a disciplinary process that regulates the actions of individuals so that they publish with the frequency and effect desired by the platform.

Regimes of Visibility on Social Media Platforms

The idea that the media can work as a disciplinary power is, of course, not new. It has been well explored, for example, by authors investigating reality makeover programmes (Heller, 2006; Miller, 2008; Weber, 2009; Deller, 2015; Skeggs, 2015). While creators of this type of show frequently highlight its democratizing role as provider of media visibility for ordinary people from different walks of life, researchers on the subject also point to its use as taste, behavioural and even body regulator. Philips (2005), for example, claims that makeover shows reinforce cultural hierarchies, which are usually regulated by designated experts, like psychologists, fashionistas, lifestyle gurus, chefs, home decorators and so forth. Moreover, Weber argues that makeover programmes engage in a process of 'affective domination', in which 'subjects are disciplined into citizenry through a combination of shaming and love power that reinforces divisions between the abject alienation of Before and the normative celebration of After' (Weber, 2009, p. 40). The media serve not only as a translator but also as 'author of cultural identities' (Turner, 2010, p. 7).

Such discussions frequently focus on the disciplinary power of the media in framing what are the 'good' or 'appropriate' uses of culture in several fields. The importance of this disciplinary power, nevertheless, transcends a form of middle-class pedagogy which penalizes working-class taste. Media in general, and social media platforms in particular, also work as a moulding force that acts in the formation of psychological, emotional and behavioural dispositions aligned with neoliberal ideologies. The subject who is always connected is situated as an entrepreneur of the self who has to learn how to self-represent on social media in an authentic manner (Illouz, 2011), while their social relations are becoming colonized by data relations following economic logics (Couldry and Mejias, 2019a).

Differently from traditional media, which have clear institutional boundaries delimiting who represents and who is represented, social media platforms make the demarcation lines much thinner. After all, the users are themselves responsible for how they are made visible and recognizable online. But that does not mean that this differentiation does not exist – quite the opposite. As Thumim (2012) argues, self-representation on social media is always connected to an idea of mediation. She suggests, for example, that the simple understanding by regular users that self-representation on digital platforms 'will be there forever' provokes, in itself, a range of responses from them (Thumim, 2012, p. 11).

In order to reflect on the impacts of datafied platforms in processes of social recognition it is, thus, key to understand how such platforms have an influence on the way individuals self-represent in the contemporary world. It is argued here that the desire to be seen and recognized as worthy subjects through social media practices cannot be divorced from the emergence of specific regimes of individual emotion and self-regulation.

From Erasmus of Rotterdam to Whindersson Nunes: a brief account of the changing regimes of visibility

In *The Civilizing Process*, German sociologist Norbert Elias discusses the transition in modes of behaviour from the Middle Ages to court society (Elias, 2000). From the sixteenth century onwards the concept of civilization gained a meaning more similar to the one contemporarily in vogue. In his account, civilization, like its ancestor *civilité*, has to do with certain forms of behaviour in society. According to Elias, the best starting-point to understand these changes is the book *De Civilitate Morum Puerilium* ('On Civility in Boys'), published by Erasmus of Rotterdam in 1530. Written in a simple and direct manner, the book by Erasmus was an instant success. It was reprinted thirty times in the first six years of its original publication and translated into several languages in the decades that followed. The book clearly met a social need of the time. *De Civilitate Morum Puerilium* was an educational manual for boys, which taught how to behave in public, mostly focusing on 'outward bodily propriety' (Elias, 2000, p. 48). It reflected a growing preoccupation with the emergence of new mental and emotional structures, which constitute the fabric of the modern subject that followed. The treatise instructed in how to conduct oneself, to carry one's body, to compose facial expressions and so on. Erasmus suggests, for example, that 'the looks of those prone to anger are too sharp' and that 'if your look shows a calm mind and respectful amiability, that is best' (Elias, 2000, p. 49).

In fact, *De Civilitate Morum Puerilium* is a manual instructing how to behave as much as how not to behave. In relation to the latter, it conveys, for instance, that civilized individuals should avoid bizarre styles of walking, not move back and forth on the chair and restrain, when it does not affect the health, natural sounds of the body in front of other people. The work addresses the entire range of human conduct of social life, and exposes a general preoccupation with how someone is perceived by others in respect to the condition of their body habitus. Some forms of behaviour not considered inappropriate in the Middle Ages, for example, slowly came to provoke institutionalized feelings of distaste or shame (Elias, 2000, p. 108).

Elias's description of *De Civilitate Morum Puerilium* came to my mind when I researched an online course for future social media influencers offered by Brazilian YouTube creator Whindersson Nunes. Nunes is one of the most influential Brazilian creators, with tens of millions of followers on each of the major social media platforms. It was on YouTube, however, that Whindersson initiated his successful career as a character making fun of ordinary situations in daily life and producing parodies of music videos. The insights used in his YouTube channel, which, in 2023, had more than 44 million subscribers, were the basis for a series of paid tutorials aimed at wannabe creators, who were willing to spend around £100 to have access to his expertise.

Divided into several thematic modules, the complete course includes over seventy videos and a number of files with written material detailing what a person should do in order to become a successful creator. The material has three overarching themes: how to produce videos of a good technical quality; how to take advantage of social media algorithms; how to self-represent on social media, especially on video formats. The last two themes are particularly interesting here, as they are intended to be a kind of manual of conduct on how the individual should behave when using datafied platforms. Like Erasmus of Rotterdam's treatise, Nunes' advice is directed at modes and regulation of emotions. Both provide instructions on how to be favourably perceived by others. What is at stake in Nunes' programme, however, is not necessarily the presentation of an idea

Regimes of Visibility on Social Media Platforms

of civility, but rather the ability to be recognized as a subject who deserves attention. Greater media visibility replaces civility as the main concern related to how someone is perceived by others.

But visibility, more than ever, needs to be negotiated with social media platforms. And this is exactly the second theme of the Whindersson course. The creator dedicates several lessons to the presentation of strategies on how to behave as much as how not to behave when dealing with algorithms (videos 2, 6 and 7).[19] He explains, for example, why a YouTuber should not 'flood' the platform with too many videos (video 1). In his assessment, the platform algorithm does not favour users who post an excessive amount of content within a short period of time (videos 1 and 4). Nunes also discusses strategies for creators to address YouTube's supposed preference for longer periods of audience viewing of each video (video 6). The point here is not to discuss whether Nunes' understanding of YouTube and other platforms' algorithms is correct. The objective, instead, is to draw attention to his preoccupation with teaching media practices which are, in theory, perceived favourably by the platforms.

The main focus of his teachings, nevertheless, is related to the third grand theme of the course, which is how to self-represent on social media. Nunes provides many strategies for winning the sympathy of the audience. He proposes, for instance, the use of metaphors in the videos (video 12), argues for tactics combining audience provocation and self-depreciation (video 14), discusses the use of punchlines (videos 15 and 16) and comic distortions (videos 15 and 20), and advocates the breaking of expectations of the audience (video 15). But perhaps his most repeated advice is for creators and digital influencers to be authentic. When presenting themselves on social media, he says, creators should show their 'originality'; they should avoid being influenced by others. 'You have to be yourself!' pontificates Whindersson Nunes in the second video of his online course. It is not difficult to see the irony here. Nunes develops a very elaborate online tutorial telling people not to be influenced by others, apart from him, of course.

This contradiction is very telling of the challenges faced by individuals nowadays. People want to be recognized as worthy subjects and to have their deeds valued by others. In order to do that, however, they have to become visible on social media news feeds and, at the same time, provoke reactions from friends and followers. According to Nunes, this can be achieved if the person behaves authentically, whatever the idea of authenticity means for him.

In fact, the rise of an ideal of authenticity is a hallmark of modernity (Trilling, 1972). In *The Ethics of Authenticity*, for instance, Taylor (1991) associates the growing importance given to this ideal with a search for a 'self determining freedom'. He reiterates the importance of the role played by Rousseau in the eighteenth century in advancing the notion that 'I am free when I decide for myself what concerns me, rather than being shaped by external influences' (Taylor, 1991, p. 27). The demand to be true to oneself while, at the same time, following certain codes of conduct in order to be valued in society is a puzzle constantly confronting contemporary media culture. There are a number of works investigating the development of strategies by celebrities, creators and reality show participants who want to be perceived as authentic individuals (for example,

Marshall, 1997; Freire Filho, 2012; Campanella, 2013; Balleys et al., 2020; Jermyn, 2021; Reade, 2021).

The seeds of this dilemma can, perhaps, be found in what Elias calls the 'antithesis of *Kultur* and *Zivilisation*' (Elias, 2000, p. 9). He is referring to the way Germans related to their own identity in the late eighteenth and early nineteenth century. Around that time, the country was not yet unified, royal courts were not central to society, and an emerging self-assured bourgeoisie was responsible for the development of a novel sense of national identity through the arts, literature and culture in general. For Elias, that early concept of culture (*Kultur*) is connected to the world of the spirit, to nature, to the arts and to the individual sensibility. At a personal level, culture has to do with emotion and to things related to the heart. In this sense, it is something profound, to be experienced by the inner self. Ultimately, it connects to the notion of individual authenticity and self-expression.

The valorization of the idea of culture was a response to the rival ideal of civilization, which dominated English and French court society. The concept of civilization gives greater emphasis to what is common to all human beings, instead of putting a focus on original expressiveness. Also, in court society, the individual had to use the mask of virtue, to be polite and to show gentle manners in order to be regarded as worthy (Elias, 2000, p. 34). In the civilizing project, form is more important than content. For that reason, civilization was described by German philosophers and writers of the time, like Kant and Goethe, as superficial and inauthentic.

This dispute of ideals also reflected the power struggles within each society. Court society, where the ideals of civilization took form, was centred around the figure of the monarch. In the palace, everything was to be seen. It was an environment involved in rituals and constant exposure. The perfection of the manners and appearance of the aristocracy was an unspoken strategy to show superiority over others (Burke, 1994). Self-discipline was initially an attribute of the nobility, but slowly became aspired to by larger segments of bourgeois society. To be civilized started to mean more than to have greater control of the body habitus. It also became related to the management of one's emotions. In court society, a man who masters his environment 'suppresses his ill temper, disguises his passions, disavows his heart, acts against his feelings', writes La Bruyère (Elias, 2000, p. 399). In a nutshell, one could say that the idea of *civilité* had, in its origins, to do with visibility, rationality, ordinariness and control, while *Kultur* was connected to emotions, inner-orientation, experience and individual singularity.

I want to argue here that the desire to develop rationalized strategies to make an individual appear authentic in the media in general is not only a difficult problem to solve, but also an enterprise reflecting a contradiction, which has its origins in this opposition described by Elias. In a way, Whindersson Nunes' formula for a successful representation of authenticity on YouTube is an incursion into this terrain. It can be described as the combination of an ethics of authenticity, on one hand, with court society's 'theatricality ... and the competitive organization of power and social mobility around the strategic projection of symbolically constituted identity' (Van Krieken, 2012, p. 16), on the other. The problem faced by celebrities, social media creators, influencers and, increasingly, also by ordinary people who want to gain recognition on social media is, in the first place, to understand how to better project a self-image that is valued by admirers and followers, and that is seen, in some sense, as unique.

When discussing the historical transformations that led to the modern phenomenon of celebrity and democratization of fame, Van Krieken (2012) stresses the formation and evolution of Elias's court society. The latter, characterized by its theatricality and performativity, was connected to the emergence of specific mental and emotional structures linked to the civilizing project, as can be seen in the work published by Erasmus of Rotterdam in the sixteenth century.

But, while performativity and management of emotions are still part of what Van Krieken describes as modern celebrity society, Wouters (2007) argues that changes in relations between individuals and groups, combined with psychic transformations taking place within people in the late nineteenth and twentieth centuries onwards, modified how people self-regulated their personality. For him, the diminishing of social inequalities and greater social integration in western countries led to a general shift towards informalization of modes of behaviour. Gradually, power was becoming less associated with self-restraint and emotional concealment. On the contrary, the greater interdependence of social classes made people more open about discussing and externalizing their feelings. According to Wouters (2007, p. 6), 'expressing social and psychic distance, whether pertaining to people of different social class, age, or gender, [increasingly] had to be done in relatively cautious and concealed ways'. In short, Wouters describes this new demand for informalization of modes of behaviour as 'a constraint to be unconstrained, at ease, and authentic' (Wouters, 2007, p. 4).

Both Elias and Wouters describe changes in regimes of self-regulation throughout history. But, while the former puts his focus on transformations taking place between the fifteenth and the nineteenth centuries in Western Europe, the latter picks up where Elias leaves off and advances through to the early twenty-first century. We should not, however, view their insights in any schematic shape or form that delimits types of emotional and bodily habitus throughout time, but rather as an indication of slow transformations of how individuals relate to their social environment: firstly taking place in specific groups and places like the French courts, before expanding to larger segments of society and different parts of the world. Their works point to changes which are analysed through a *sociogenesis* as well as *psychogenesis* perspective, i.e. with a lens on the relation between social groups and individuals, and on the management of individuals' emotions and how they 'relate to themselves'.

What is significant for our discussion is to emphasize that the changes described by these authors are directly connected to shifts in power relations occurring during that epoch. Wouters, for example, showed that etiquette and manners books published in the last one hundred years or so were progressively directed towards a wider audience, which reflected the ascent of larger groups of society to positions of visibility and, in many cases, of power. This process of social integration, also reflected in P. D. Marshall's citizenship evolution model (Marshall, 1997), tended to blur social dividing lines based on class, race, age or ethnicity (Wouters, 2007, p. 52). Open displays of superiority and inferiority gave way to an expansion of regimes of manners and emotions. The guides and books researched by Wouters generally advised people to be more informal towards the other, even if they belong to different social spheres. Of course, this does not mean that social, ethnic, sex and race barriers disappeared. They may have diminished since court society, but were still there, though in a more silent and ambiguous fashion.

In fact, Wouters also explores how these publications articulated new anxieties that stemmed from the growing emancipation and social integration of distinct groups of people in the countries examined. The books analysed by him frequently offered 'double' advice: on the one hand, they championed friendly manners and respect towards people in disadvantaged social positions; on the other, they accentuated the importance of conducts that delineated class borders (Wouters, 2007, p. 39). Despite temporal and national fluctuations identified in the trends described in his work, Wouters offers some interesting insights in relation to what books on etiquette and manners expected from individuals in terms of psychological and emotional habitus throughout the twentieth century until the dawn of the internet.

Self-representation on social media platforms

When discussing transformations in regimes of visibility of the self, and how these changes affect the way individuals are valued by others, it is useful to distinguish between two related ideas commonly associated with these regimes: performance of the self and self-representation. The former has its origins in Goffman's theatrical metaphor of backstage and frontstage (Goffman, 1983). For him, individuals manage differently the impressions they produce on others, depending on the social circumstances in place. According to this perspective, individuals ultimately want to be believed and have their appearance and attitude accepted by others. Goffman's theory on backstage and frontstage has been adopted by media and communication researchers interested, for example, in analyses of performances of reality show participants (Andacht, 2003; Campanella, 2012) and, more recently, in works investigating practices (Livingstone, 2008) and performative ruptures (Polivanov and Carrera, 2019) on social media.

Self-representation, on the other hand, involves the circulation of symbolic forms. Thumim (2012, p. 6) proposes that 'when someone produces a self-representation they produce a bounded text, however fleeting and ephemeral that text might be'. This is different from Goffman's theory that we all continually perform the self, even if sometimes in an unconscious manner. Thumim argues that both concepts coexist and that the exact notion of self-representation 'raises questions about the mediation of a textual object', which can generate later engagement.

It is equally important to reflect on the differences between the concepts of self-representation and representation. The latter implicitly presupposes that a person or group of people will represent another set of people. The popularization in the twentieth century of mass media such as radio, television and film has prompted many discussions on the issue of media representation, especially on the representation of ordinary people (Turner, 2010). Furthermore, chapter 2 showed how the media are seen as key sites in contemporary struggles for recognition, especially when it comes to struggles around positive media representation of disfranchised and minority groups. In fact, the issue of representation is central to gender, race, postcolonial and cultural studies in general (Ang, 1985; Brunsdon, 1995; Hall and Du Gay, 1996; Said, 2003).

Self-representation, instead, assumes that 'people are doing it for themselves' (Thumim, 2012, p. 8); it implies, at least in theory, a notion of freedom and choice. In this sense, to self-represent would mean that the person representing and being represented is less bounded by external forms of power. The issue, however, is a bit more complicated.

For instance, Elias and Wouters argue that any form of self-representation is somehow constrained by historical and social regimes of self-regulation. The capacity of the individual to show specific types of emotion, to relate to their own body in particular ways and to express or avoid intimacy towards others changes over time, and from place to place. In this respect, Illouz (2011) proposes that the major sociological narratives of modernity can also be read from the perspective of the transformation of feelings and affects. Simmel's description of the blasé attitude, marked by a sense of indifference towards others and a tepid sensitivity for the distinctions between things, is an example of a narrative related to the rise of the metropolis and to the money economy (Simmel, 1973).

Affections and emotions, Illouz claims, are semi-conscious and highly internalized aspects of individuals' actions (Illouz, 2011, p. 10). Affections are frequently described as a type of psychological entity – which is true – but she contends that they are as much social and cultural entities as well. When individuals self-represent, be it on a TV show or on social media, they follow regimes of visibility that are sometimes not very evident to them. The very desire to self-represent on media, of any kind, is already an act of recognition and adherence to the dispersed power of media, a power which interferes in the divisions of the social order, as proposed by Couldry (2005, 2012).

Illouz (2011) is particularly interested in understanding how capitalism has walked hand in hand with the creation of an affective culture aimed at increasing corporate profits. She points to the development of therapeutic discourses, based on the psychoanalytic tradition, to harness feelings and affects capable of making individuals more productive in their working environments. She also contends that modern identity is increasingly enacted through personal narratives of self-realization, which she describes as 'narratives of recognition' (Illouz, 2011, p. 12). In her perspective, middle-class men and women in western societies have built personal and professional relations that mix public and private spheres, distinguished by a type of rationalized and commoditized feeling that is also marked by a desire for self-fulfilment. The process of identity construction, according to Illouz, unfolds more intensely on internet platforms responsible for the construction of a public emotional self that desires recognition and that frequently precedes the construction of private sphere relations. For instance, when analysing dating sites, like Match.com, she describes their demand for users to self-represent, a process in which these users have to engage in a 'vast process of reflexive self-observation, introspection, self-labelling and articulation of tastes and opinions' (Illouz, 2011, p. 111).

Originally writing in the mid-2000s, Illouz notes, back then, that the internet promotes a textualization of subjectivity in which the self is 'externalized and objectified through visual means of representation and language' (Illouz, 2011, p. 113). As a result, the individual is required to concentrate on their own selves and on their ideal selves. For Honneth this demand for a kind of self-commodification of the individual produces the risk of 'self-reification'. In his words, 'the more a subject is exposed to demands for self-portrayal, the more he [sic] will tend to experience all of his desires and intensions as arbitrarily manipulable things' (Honneth, 2008, p. 83). Honneth believes that this propensity for self-reification might increase as the 'institutions of self-portrayal' become more present in daily life. Although both Illouz and Honneth explore the consequences of such dynamics primarily as they appear through dating sites in the mid-2000s, this is, in fact, a broader phenomenon that today comprises social media in general.

Or, social media as dispositives of self-representation

Thumim argues that any form of self-representation is mediated by three dimensions: textual, cultural and institutional. The textual dimension, in the case of social media, is related to how self-representation is expressed. As an example, she mentions videos published on YouTube by feminist activists challenging dominant representations of women, which use, in the cases analysed, to-camera short interventions reacting to mainstream media (Thumim, 2012, p. 150). Thumim suggests that this type of mediation may constitute a challenge to dominant negative representations of feminists. She also refers to the Facebook status update architecture and how it stimulates its users to express feelings in no more than two sentences. This form of textual mediation can have, in its turn, the consequence of levelling up types of self-representation which do not have much in common, like the expression of political inclinations, shopping habits and food tastes. Mediations are contests for power, and the architectures behind the textual dimension of such mediations also reflect the interests at stake, whether of the users of the platforms or of the platforms themselves and the economic interests they represent.

In regard to the cultural dimension, for instance, Thumim confers special attention to media literacy and how it gives power to individuals in relation to their own representation. As an illustration, she discusses the ways in which users of social media like Facebook constantly make decisions around the types of photos they use to self-represent, when to change these photos, with whom they share them, etc. For her, the level of media literacy of social media users is central in the processes of cultural mediation moulding practices of self-representation on these platforms (Thumim, 2012, p. 149).

I want to propose here, nevertheless, that particularly in the case of social media platforms these dimensions of mediation should be analysed in tandem with the institutional dimension. Traditional media are not constituted through the idea of self-representation, although some reality-based programmes may rely on it. Social media like Instagram and Facebook, on the other hand, frequently affirm that they are all about socializing; however, in order to do that, users have, in one way or another, to self-represent. There are, of course, people who go to great lengths in their attempts to avoid giving away traces of their 'true selves' when using social media. But, even in these situations, the online identities being represented can also be seen as forms of representation of desired or ideal selves (Kiziltunali, 2016). In other words, self-representation is not only a central feature of social media use, but the cultural and textual aspects of these platforms are ingrained in their institutional mediation.

When Honneth suggests that 'institutions of self-portrayal' are becoming more prevalent in contemporary society, and that they promote the development of 'reifying behaviour', he is not making a prognostic assertion based on empirical research. Instead, he wants to demarcate the logics informing plausible social changes resulting from the dissemination of dispositives of self-representation like social media platforms (Honneth, 2008, p. 84). These dispositives carry specific rationalities that act in the creation and naturalization of a type of datafied habitus, as briefly discussed in the first chapter.

Dispositives are understood here as technologies, principles and logics that intertwine, mould, capture, guide and determine the gestures, conducts and opinions of contemporary subjectivities (Agamben, 2009, p. 40). I use this concept, as developed by Agamben, to discuss the formation of the necessary requirements for recognition on datafied platforms. Originally proposed by Foucault (1979b) with the aim of describing the role of modern institutions, such as the school, the prison, the legal system and the factory, in the formation of the subject of disciplinary power, the concept was taken up by Agamben in his effort to think about other forms of dispersed power present in contemporary society. In this sense, I want to reflect on the architecture, operating logics and characteristics of dispositives that act directly on the subject's self-realization, enabling them to be perceived as a useful member of society. Social media platforms are forms of power for several reasons: among them their capacity to create a social space, with its own rules, where people increasingly look forward to self-represent and to be recognized.

It is important to observe, nonetheless, that social media platforms differ in their type of demand for self-representation. Facebook and Instagram, for example, offer several functionalities specifically aimed at allowing their users to self-represent through the creation of media traces like short texts, photos, the use of social plug-ins, etc., which can be scrutinized by others while offering aspects of identity valued by the person self-representing. The very act of publishing a selfie on Instagram, for instance, has become a common way of creating individual representation and, in the case of group selfies, social performances (Humphreys, 2018, p. 88). It is thus impossible to dissociate self-representation from socialization on these platforms. And although other platforms, like YouTube[20] and TikTok, describe themselves more as spaces for self-expression and creativity, they also produce textual mediations which articulate the identity of their creators and consumers in general. A crucial aspect shared by these dispositives, nonetheless, is their data-driven architectures, which transform the social into information geared at generating more information and profit.

In the example discussed earlier in this chapter, YouTube creator Whindersson Nunes offers in his online course some valuable advice on how to self-represent on YouTube and take advantage of the platform algorithm in order to achieve greater visibility. Nunes discusses the use of hashtags and proposes optimizing video lengths and frequency of posting as well as other strategies aimed at exploiting the data-driven principles behind the platforms. Some of the basic tenets of these architectures, however, are widely known by users, and sometimes proactively shared by the platforms themselves.

This is the case with YouTube, which developed an initiative called The Creator Academy aimed at YouTubers who want to gain greater reach on the platform. As part of this project, the platform launched a series of videos called YouTube Search & Discovery specifically dedicated to teaching creators how to optimize their content in order to become more easily found by other users. Araújo argues that this project should be seen as a manifestation of what he calls the *algorithm norm*, described as a 'relationship between producers and the news feed classification systems in which a range of behaviours and actions are considered to be legitimate' (Araújo, 2018, p. 14). When analysing YouTube Search & Discovery videos, Araújo suggests that the platform tries to persuade its users that its algorithm just follows the public's interests – in an apparent effort to make the logics of its inner workings and decision-making processes invisible. The author explains that the videos constituting the series reduce the complexity of the YouTube algorithm by presenting it as a simple and singular entity that barely has any kind of agency. According to one of the videos analysed, called The Algorithm,[21] YouTube looks at 'titles, thumbnails, descriptions and how other viewers seem to be enjoying it' to make content on the platform discoverable by the public. YouTube's narrative gives the impression that it is the public that is principally responsible for categorizing all the actions taking place on the platform.

At the same time, however, these tutorial videos propose the normalization of specific practices that should mark the relationship between creators and their audience. The former are advised to introduce 'call-to-actions' in their videos, asking their public to leave comments, watch the videos to the end, activate notifications, follow the creator's channel, etc. (Araújo, 2021, p. 37). Creators are valued by the algorithm according to their capacity to retain users for longer periods on the platform and to make them return to watch more videos and spend more time there. For Magalhães (2019, p. 72), social media platforms such as Facebook produce an 'algorithmic visibility regime' in which end users are expected to produce certain media practices, whilst not having access to the platform's infrastructural resources which are responsible for reading and datafying the users' actions.

Naturally, the visibility regimes that Magalhães and Araújo discuss have marked differences from those analysed throughout this chapter. This does not mean, however, that it is not possible to think about how tutorials, courses and formulae recently created to achieve success in social media revisit problems identified by authors such as Elias and Wouters, who researched books and manuals on social conduct, some of them written nearly five centuries ago, and which sharply reflect the values and expectations of their times. The book by Erasmus, for example, gives concreteness to a regime of visibility that was slowly taking shape: a result of the rise of the modern individual and the idea of civilization that accompanies it. Whindersson Nunes' course, as discussed earlier, combines the theatricality that spans the idea of *civilité* present in Erasmus with the search for an ideal of authenticity, while simultaneously proposing an informalization of the relationship between the creator and their audience. The search for media recognition by digital influencers, celebrities and, increasingly, by the common individual can be read, in a certain sense, as the materialization of the dilemmas resulting from the combination of these regimes of visibility.

Magalhães and Araújo, in turn, bring a new element to this discussion, namely, the problem of the algorithm in social media platforms. The importance of thinking about the algorithm as a dispositive of power lies precisely in its ability to interfere in the production of the sensible (Rancière, 2009) and the categorization and hierarchization of the social. These dispositives invest in the creation of a datafied habitus linked to emotional, psychological and behavioural dispositions that naturalize self-representation and, more broadly, a connection with the social *through* the use of quantified parameters that produce economic value for the platforms and for the users themselves. This type of habitus also reflects an affective visibility regime that, as some researchers have recently demonstrated (Rieder et al., 2018), has contributed to the radicalization of individual expressions of emotion and opinion on platforms, and to the phenomenon generically known as 'cancel culture'. The issue is particularly important since the visibility regimes created in the context of datafied social media have consequences in the processes of social recognition, even if the platforms obscure the complexity of their role as dispositives of power.

Recognition in the Age of Social Media

Recognition theory as an analytical tool

There are, of course, several works problematizing how social media platforms relate to processes of self-realization and identity formation which do not draw on recognition theory. Karppi (2018) and Paasonen (2021), for instance, explore the ambivalences of such technologies in relation to their capacity to foster social equality, whilst, at the same time, relying on 'affective manipulation within data capitalism' (Paasonen, 2021, p. 14). The economic and technological frameworks described by them and other researchers (like Zuboff, 2019) are enacted by algorithms, which have to constantly decide '*what*[22] is relevant, in a generic sense, and *who* is the user, so that this generic rule about relevance can be applied individually' (Araújo and Magalhães, 2018, p. 4). In this context, recognition theory, especially in Honneth's approach, offers an interesting entry point to the debate because of its normative effort to understand the formation of personal and social value, and its preoccupation with the constitution of identity.

4
The Demand for New Dispositions

What is datafied habitus, anyway? It is argued here that datafied habitus centres around the demands for constant social media presence, the cultivation of specific emotional dispositions, as discussed in chapter 3, and the assimilation of neoliberal ideals such as flexibility, adaptability and self-entrepreneurship. The chapter, nonetheless, does not offer a schematic description of the concept, as datafied habitus refers to dispositions linked to constantly changing online practices, which can take diverse shapes and hues. In short, datafied habitus has to do with structures of perception and systems of being, acting and thinking related to social media platforms. These structures and systems are discussed in this chapter alongside the socioeconomic environment that shapes their development.

Successful digital influencers, algorithm experts (Bishop, 2020) and even the datafied platforms provide formulae for how individuals should self-represent in the media to increase their visibility and be favourably recognized. These formulae prioritize the development of psychological, emotional and behavioural predispositions that, according to these models, should be internalized by the person in their connection with the world rather than mere suggestions on how to perform on social media. Although the simple search for visibility is a fundamental issue in today's world, as concepts such as *visibility capital* (Heinich, 2012), *circuits of visibility* (Hegde, 2011) and *economies of visibility* (Banet-Weiser, 2015) demonstrate, the struggle for recognition pervades a significant portion of online media practices, even if this is not explicitly stated.

Posting selfies on Instagram and other social media sites, for instance, is a practice widely connected with the pursuit of personal recognition, and transcends demographic and cultural boundaries. Nemer and Freeman's (2015) research on selfies in Brazilian favelas, for example, demonstrates that the practice of taking selfies facilitates residents' capacity to enter social circles within the researched community, as well as the communication of joyful moments in the otherwise difficult daily lives of these individuals. Selfies are, in this sense, understood as a product of social empowerment within the disadvantaged groups analysed. In a similar vein, Nikunen (2019) uses the term 'selfie activism' to describe the practice of refugees taking selfies for the social media campaign 'Once I Was a Refugee' in Finland in 2015. For Nikunen, the opportunity to post selfies accompanied by brief captions that help describe some of the refugees' life experiences provided a 'space of appearance' that introduced fresh voices into the hostile political atmosphere of that country's public discourse. The aforementioned empirical studies distance themselves from others that traditionally associate selfies with a 'culture of narcissism' (Barakat, 2014), often connected to recent transformations in western subjectivities (Lash, 1991; Sennett, 2001). While acknowledging the potential for new agency arising from forms of 'selfie citizenship', Kuntsman nevertheless cautions about the risks that such practices, which are often regulated by 'large-scale dataisation', pose to the maintenance of a sense of collectivity and citizenship. The practice of selfies involves, in certain circumstances, the construction of privileges and types of capital that are far from universally shared (Kuntsman, 2017, p. 17).

Of course, I do not want to reduce an individual's pursuit of recognition on social media platforms, which I have designated as datafied recognition, to the phenomenon of selfies. Selfies are but one of the many types of self-representation in social media that may contribute to generating self-confidence and self-esteem, which are vital to individual recognition and self-realization. In fact, it is challenging, to say the least, to distinguish precisely which everyday self-representation practices on social media have the pursuit of social recognition as their main objective. In certain ways, posting selfies on Instagram, humorous videos on TikTok or comments complimenting professional accomplishments on Facebook, to mention a few examples, are actions that share, to varying degrees, this purpose. Ultimately, they are practices that entail conscious, and sometimes unconscious, decisions about what individuals wish to reveal about their everyday lives, choices and worldviews – practices that are subject to frequent scrutiny and evaluation by others. The centrality that social plug-ins such as liking, sharing and following have gained in the experience of utilizing datafied social media platforms demonstrates the significance that evaluative processes play in contemporary forms of self-representation and sociability. This issue is especially pertinent due to the fact that these evaluation processes, particularly their quantitative aspects, have direct effects on the subject's capacity to be recognized and consequently permit the production of various types of capital, whether symbolic or material. But creating such a subjectivity that is connected to a person's ability to produce highly valued forms of self-representation on social media comes at a price.

Duffy and Pooley (2019) contribute to thinking about these costs in their adaptation to the modern media milieu of Lowenthal's (2006) foundational work on entertainment culture in the first half of the twentieth century. The model subject that stands out in today's mediated biographies would no longer be the 'idols of consumption' of the early 1940s or even the 'idols of production', which preceded them by a few decades according to Lowenthal, but rather the 'idols of promotion'. Duffy and Pooley claim that these new idols come to dominate media forms of self-representation by acting as author-producers of their own narratives and careers. While inviting their fans to emulate their successful examples in their media relations, these new idols experience a constant feeling of anxiety and precariousness as a result of their dependence on the ever-changing and demanding logic of digital platforms, as also described by Glatt (2022).

According to Biressi (2017), the rise in popularity of selfies and other self-representational phenomena in digital media is related to the emergence of a morality that encourages the improvement of the subject via personal projects in the media sphere. Biressi contends, based on substantial empirical research, that selfies serve as a bridge between the subject's personal biography and their social media profiles in many instances, providing various types of advantages professionally (Biressi, 2017, p. 132). In this sense, she argues that work-related selfies serve as evidence of passion for work, convey self-confidence and ambition, and consequently enhance prospects for career advancement. Also taking Leo Lowenthal's seminal work as a starting point (Lowenthal, 2006), today's so-called 'idol of self-production' represents an ideal subject who exploits 'the idiom of celebrity, via their engagement with selfie culture' (Biressi, 2017, p. 141) to become 'good' citizens.

Again, we observe in Biressi a correlation between citizenship and media self-representation practices, manifested here by the selfie. Is this kind of citizenship, however, attainable for everyone? Is it reasonable to believe that social media platforms constitute a broad and democratic environment in which individuals may be recognized as full citizens in their differences and similarities? The issue of access to citizenship is extensive, and I do not want to imply that it can be reduced to the subject's active presence on social media. Yet, this relationship between citizenship and the media has been increasingly developed by communication and media studies scholars (Weber, 2009; De Oliveira and Nunes, 2011; Kuntsman, 2017; Barassi, 2019).

It is my contention that the growing prevalence of emotional and psychosocial dispositions forming a specific self-consciousness linked to social media platforms, which can be understood as a distinct habitus, legitimizes practices of sociability permeated by economic, political and material logics that regulate the media infrastructure. The pursuit of datafied recognition, in particular, naturalizes the assumption that social media are a critical feature of the subject's self-realization, allowing them to be perceived as a useful member of society.

Dispositions for a 'subordinate inclusion'

Bourdieu defines habitus as a system of dispositions and methods of being, acting and thinking. According to the French sociologist, habitus is 'a system of *long-lasting* (rather than permanent) schemes or schemata or structures of perception, conception and action' (Bourdieu, 2002, p. 43). First and foremost, the concept refers to something unnatural, something learnt and sustained within a shared social experience, often using pedagogical means. Habitus operates as a structuring structure capable of transforming objective structures while itself being restructured.

Although Bourdieu highlights the application of habitus within different cultural fields, whether in taste formation or in artistic practice (2000, 2002), the concept may also be considered with respect to the production of citizenship. This is Souza's (2003) proposal, with the introduction of the concept of primary habitus. Primary habitus, as outlined in chapter 1, refers to the psychological, emotional and behavioural dispositions that allow a person to be recognized and constitute their self as a whole citizen. In contrast to Bourdieu's examination of the construction of taste and its relationship to the individual's class expression, Souza seeks to understand which particular configurations pervade the formation of self-confidence, self-respect and self-esteem in the contemporary subject. In his view, these sentiments are required for a person to be regarded as wholly integrated into a capitalist society. In other words, by shifting the focus to individual dispositions, Souza complexifies traditional models of citizenship studies, which portray drawn-out and incremental processes (with occasional setbacks) of struggle to consolidate the civil, political, social and cultural dimensions of citizenship (Marshall, 1950; Pakulski, 1997). The Brazilian sociologist highlights the individual's productive capacity in terms of personal dispositions as an indispensable requisite for social recognition. Analysing these dispositions, according to Lahire (2004, p. 27), 'presupposes an interpretative work to account for behaviors, practices, opinions, etc. It is about bringing to light the principle or principles that generated the apparent diversity of practices.'

In his empirical study of the genesis of what he terms the 'hard-worker class' in Brazil, Souza finds three primary dispositions in the life experiences of his research subjects. The first disposition, *self-overcoming*, refers to the proclivity for sentiments and actions aimed at overcoming an adverse socioeconomic condition (Souza, 2012, p. 96). By analysing the participants' stories, Souza determined the factors that led to the emergence of certain dispositions. These included the ability and willingness for professional learning via experience, the readiness to engage in future planning, the acquisition of 'superior' consumer goods, and the development of positive personal and professional images, among others. Workers' accounts of their dreams, ambitions, personal relationships, and the manner in which they connect to their day-to-day job revealed these inclinations related to self-overcoming.

The second disposition Souza identified, the *economic disposition*, pertains to what Bourdieu (1979, p. 4) refers to as 'the spirit of calculation and forecasting'. That is, it is the subject's predisposition to use economic calculation in their everyday activities while valuing cost-saving attitudes. Particularly, it was highlighted, for instance, in the testimonies of people who described their efforts to save money in order to start a service-based business or small enterprise.

The *administrative disposition*, Souza's third and final finding on the new Brazilian hard worker class, is directly dependent on the first two. It is connected to the effective management of a small business, such as coordination and planning. Ultimately, the administrative disposition relates to how individuals position themselves in the world, their economic rationality and managerial organization (Souza, 2012, p. 97).

Souza provides various instances of how these dispositions emerged in the accounts examined. In one passage, a research participant states that he 'tries to improve the appearance and the environment in which he provides services for his clients', 'in business, appearance is everything'. In another instance, which would be associated with the disposition of self-overcoming, a participant relates that 'after a lot of work and with that experience (which set him apart) he received a promotion. He became "in charge"; he speaks of this with great pride' (ibid., p. 99).

According to Lahire (2004), dispositions cannot be evaluated just on the basis of a particular event or practice. Examining the dispositions that comprise habitus entails observing a 'series of behaviors, attitudes and practices that are coherent' (Lahire, 2004, p. 27). It is the author's contention that processes of socialization

The Demand for New Dispositions

and education are the sources from which a person's dispositions originate.

Similarly, Jessé Souza proposes that the dispositions identified in the investigated groups of hard workers – dispositions associated with self-control, discipline and prospective thinking – were learned both in professional settings and in the participants' own familial, educational and cultural surroundings. The Brazilian sociologist argues that such dispositions produce 'subordinate inclusion' within the current phase of capitalism. In contrast to the most vulnerable socioeconomic minorities and marginalized segments of society, this hard worker may at least be recognized as a useful member of society, although via a tenuous and unstable inclusion. While the traditional working class has historically formed community bonds and a shared sense of solidarity through spaces such as the union, class associations and/or political parties (Thompson, 1963; Freire, 2005), the current hard-working class inhabits a symbolic field of individualized action, represented by small entrepreneurs who, in general, rely on themselves for recognition.

Boltanski and Chiapello (2009) suggest that such changes have occurred mainly since the 1980s, with the development of a 'new spirit of capitalism'. The scholars identify transformations in the way exclusion is conceptualized. According to the Marxist tradition, social exclusion throughout the nineteenth century and for most of the twentieth was defined as exclusion from the field of labour, and its genesis was attributed to class exploitation. This perception started to shift after World War II, owing primarily to the economic growth enjoyed by more economically and socially developed western countries.

There was optimism at the time about a purported continuous improvement in living conditions, which many believed would result in the standardization of economic circumstances and the concomitant disappearance of social classes, particularly with respect to exploitative relations (Boltanski and Chiapello, 2009, p. 353). Boltanski and Chiapello draw on Lenoir's work to analyse how the concept of exclusion changed in the waning decades of the twentieth century. In his book *Les Exclus* ('The Excluded'), Lenoir (1974) proposes that the causes of exclusion should be attributed, primarily, to specific limitations and deficiencies of individuals, which prevent them from contributing to the production of wealth in society. In other words, capitalism and its exploitation structures are no longer seen as the source of exclusion. The excluded are no longer victims of the system, but rather victims of their own physical and mental incapacities. Exclusion is now associated with what Boltanski (1999) refers to as the 'topic of feeling', as opposed to the prior 'topic of denunciation'.

The 'exclusion paradigm's' growing connection with the network metaphor, however, is what stands out most about these transformations. According to Boltanski and Chiapello, the included individual is connected, at different levels, to other individuals and instances such as the family, the workplace and other social groups. The excluded, on the contrary, 'are those who have seen the ties that bound them to others severed, and have thus been relegated to the fringes of the network, where beings lose all *visibility*,[23] all rationale, and virtually all existence' (Boltanski and Chiapello, 2009, p. 355). The experience of the connectionist world is one of adaptability to flexible, networked labour relations and a value placed on the individual's entrepreneurial spirit. Solidarity gives way to competition and vulnerability since connections need to be continuously created to prevent exclusion.

Both Boltanski and Chiapello's and Souza's findings allude to the depersonalization of capital and the obfuscation of the labour exploitation process. The desire to be recognized as a worthy citizen and included in a productive social system demands the assimilation of psychological, emotional and behavioural dispositions that guide the values and actions of today's individuals. These dispositions, which constitute the primary habitus defined by Souza, are characterized, in short, by the incorporation of economic and connectionist aspects into the most mundane choices of daily life. However, I contend that the current deepening of the datafication of social life, which has occurred in recent decades, has incorporated dispositions into this habitus that were not apparent when Souza conducted his study in the 2000s. Some authors suggest that participation in digital platforms nowadays occurs through systematic processes of coercion (Barassi, 2019). This favours the rise of a new type of 'sharing citizen' (Chambers, 2017), who produces content and actions on social media in the hope of obtaining future individual benefits (Kuehn and Corrigan, 2013), but who, ultimately, benefits the platforms themselves economically rather than the individual or their community. In sum, despite, or maybe because of, the advancement of datafied platforms, the drive towards the precarization of citizenship and recognition production processes has intensified in recent years.

Recognition in the Age of Social Media

Beyond media literacy

Based on extensive research with small business owners, telemarketers, rural producers in single-family units, and other entrepreneurs, Souza analyses the dispositions necessary for the subject to be fully inserted into society, to be recognized in all their uniqueness, and to be treated as a productive and worthy citizen, even under precarious conditions. Ultimately, Souza sees these arrangements as part of broader economic and social transformations that weaken solidarity bonds and cast doubt on the very concept of individual freedom. Likewise, I propose in this chapter to consider whether the dispositions required for the production of recognition in datafied environments are similarly embedded in the subordinate inclusion defined by Souza, even if different terms.

Given the growth of social media over the past decade, I want to reflect on the dispositions that constitute a contemporary primary habitus necessary for the individual to have their worth recognized in everyday practices that increasingly take place in datafied environments. In contrast to Souza's empirical research, here I address these issues via the examination of works that concentrate on the role of social media platforms in the production of subjectivities. I am interested in considering whether such dispositions are effectively capable of producing citizenship and recognition in the broadest meaning of these terms, as proposed by Honneth.

Even though each person develops their own unique self-representation on each social media platform used, it is feasible to identify behavioural and emotional regimes that are valued in the logic that permeates and organizes

The Demand for New Dispositions

digital platforms. These behavioural regimes, however, should not be confused with the concept of media literacy. While Thumim (2012) acknowledges the significance of media literacy for media self-representation, the development of a habitus associated with digital media should be considered independently of media literacy. The latter is often discussed in the context of developing skills that enable children and youth to navigate a world that is more and more reliant on various forms of media (Livingstone, 2007, 2011; Borges et al., 2021).

Initially, media literacy was seen as a challenge, particularly for educators, due to the dilemmas posed by the rise of electronic and print media, such as television and newspapers, in the construction of social reality (UNESCO, 1983; Aufderheide, 1993). In the 1980s and 1990s, when the internet was still a distant reality in many people's lives, the construction of media literacy focused on the study of the creation and reception of television programmes, the acquisition of skills for content production, and, ultimately, the pursuit of an understanding of the social production of knowledge. Of course, this kind of concern was not new. It can be observed, for example, in the establishment of schools and the standardization of the written language in eighteenth-century Europe, which coincided with the expansion of the printing press and the progressive replacement of oral culture on the continent (Luke, 1989). These movements demonstrate how the emergence and consolidation of new media are constantly followed by attempts to build competencies related to them. However, the advent of the internet, with all its dynamism and complexity, has provided a new impetus to the debate on the role of media literacy in society. Livingstone's (2003) attempt to reimagine the fundamental idea of media literacy is motivated by the convergent nature of technology, which is able to combine audiovisual and printed works with the computational capabilities of the digital. According to the author, the concept reflects 'the ability to access, analyse, evaluate and create messages across a variety of contexts' (Livingstone, 2003, p. 1).

Livingstone contends that the internet is more than just a technology that aggregates traditional media or enhances the accessibility of conventional types of content. The author argues that it has the capacity to alter a society's culture and knowledge. As a consequence, the popularization of this technology requires the revision of long-held beliefs about how knowledge, authority and cognition are produced. Livingstone (2007) emphasizes the need for developing a critical awareness of internet content producers' intentions, understanding the architecture, visuals and security of these technologies, and, of course, strengthening the ability to create content in its different formats. According to scholarly research, a democratic society characterized by participatory and active citizenship necessitates internet literacy that extends beyond the technical realm, as it includes the acquisition of cultural and social capital, as well as extratextual knowledge associated with political and critical competence (Buckingham, 2007; Livingstone, 2011; Herdzina and Lauricella, 2020).

According to Jenkins et al. (2016) and Greenhow and Lewin (2016), this tendency is accentuated by the popularization of social media, which, according to Scolari (2018), necessitate critical prosumer transmedia literacy. In certain ways, the rapid creation, distribution and re-signification of content on social media platforms, along with the rising demand for

The Demand for New Dispositions

fast, visual content, have led to a revaluation of oral culture and a revived concern about media literacy. This phenomenon becomes even more obvious when one considers the increasing relevance of short videos in the content produced on social media platforms. As a direct consequence of these transformations, the rise of TikTok, the most downloaded platform in the world in 2021,[24] as well as the recent introduction of Reels on Instagram and Shorts on YouTube, points to the need for the development of specific skills related to personal communication and audiovisual production.

Media or transmedia literacy is therefore a proposal for the development of competencies that enable us to understand the consumption and production of content more extensively in various types of media. Although originally intended for children and teenagers, these competencies are necessary for individuals of all ages and social groups to be able to behave in accordance with a model of active and critical citizenship in our mediatized society.

The regimes of behaviour and emotion that comprise what I regard as the datafied habitus are distinguished by dispositions that require a prior understanding of how social media and digital platforms in general operate. The capacity to cope with the phenomenon of digital oral culture, for example, and the particularities of how it manifests itself on each social media platform are all part of the media literacy process. I can personally see a definite shift in students' abilities to produce short and medium-length videos for digital platforms in the Introduction to Audiovisual class which I have been teaching for over ten years in the Media Studies undergraduate course at Universidade Federal Fluminense, in Brazil. The content that students have created in recent years demonstrates a deeper familiarity with the audiovisual language and publishing techniques necessary to increase visibility. This is especially notable given that the topic at issue is a first-year discipline, indicating that these competencies are being learned generally even before students have a more formal engagement with the subject in the classroom. This anecdote, although lacking empirical validity, corroborates a widely held belief that young people with access to digital technologies and the internet have been improving, sometimes informally, their media literacy, at least in terms of producing content capable of garnering visibility on social media (Scolari, 2018).

However, as stated at the outset of this discussion, the strong relationship between media literacy and its corresponding ability for digital media creation and consumption should not be equated with the behavioural and emotional regimes that comprise the datafied habitus. The latter, while involving competencies mentioned in discussions about media literacy, goes much further. The datafied habitus is present in the very formation of subjectivities and in their processes of self-regulation and connection with the outward world. Given the extent and complexity of this form of habitus, it would be impossible to include all of its characteristics in a reflective work like this one. The discussions raised throughout this book nonetheless hint at avenues that help to comprehend certain facets of these dispositions.

The demand for permanent connection

A structuring disposition of this habitus is the widespread acceptance of the assumption that individuals must be constantly connected to social media platforms. Illouz (2011, p. 10) describes this kind of affective relationship with social media as constituting 'internalized and non-reflexive' actions of subjects' practices. The author contends that these actions are pre-reflexive and semi-conscious not because they are insufficiently incorporated into culture and society, but rather because they are excessively integrated into them.

Quantitative studies that illustrate the steady increase in the number of hours per day that people in various countries devote to social media demonstrate the willingness to consume and consistently publish multiple types of content, whether personal, professional, or that communicate the individual's creative expression.[25] As was already mentioned, frequent and consistent posting on social media, particularly when done by individuals with some level of media meta-capital (Couldry, 2003a), such as journalists, politicians, athletes, artists, academics or digital influencers, is frequently rewarded with a verification badge created by social media, which further encourages such practices.

The verified account is more than just a status symbol: it stands for the straightforward acquisition of power. It exacerbates what Heinich (2012) refers to as 'visibility capital', since it plays a significant part in the current hierarchical processes of publishing in digital platforms' algorithms.

Nathalie Heinich invokes the concept of social capital developed by Bourdieu (1986) as well as the issue of asymmetry in personal visibility to analyse how celebrities accumulate social relations that are convertible into economic gains. What makes this 'amplified visibility' a type of capital is its imbalance. That is, a celebrity is known by the unknown. The greater the imbalance between the number of people who know an individual and the number of people this same individual knows, the greater their capital. This positive differential is, as noted above, what Heinich calls 'visibility capital', which can be measured quantitatively and, at the same time, transformed into economic capital. The French sociologist lists many indicators created by the industry itself to measure the visibility of celebrities: the numbers in paying audiences at concerts, media attention to their public appearances, the size and number of fan clubs, the number of social media followers, and the number of search results on Google are some of them (Heinich, 2012, pp. 47–8).

This principle also applies to verified accounts on social media platforms. These accounts are given a distinct status by the platforms' algorithms, which leads to an imbalance in user visibility and increases the social capital of the verified individual. The verified account enables its comments, shares, videos, etc. to gain greater reach in news feeds where there is some kind of interaction, while these algorithms consider multiple signals and affinity scores in their decisions about the hierarchical positioning given to objects on users' timelines (Bucher, 2018). In other words, the actions produced by people with verified accounts gain, by definition, a greater voice on social media platforms. Rankings for publications that appear in social media news feeds follow certain criteria that are constantly changing. For instance, in 2022 Instagram started emphasizing algorithmically promoted content in its news feeds that was unrelated to the profiles users were following, devaluing its historical model that had valued the relationship between profiles that knew one another. Analysts claim that this would be a way for

The Demand for New Dispositions

Instagram and even Facebook, which is going through a similar transformation, to approach the TikTok news feed organization style, which has proven to be more effective in attracting and retaining users (Bhandari and Bimo, 2022).

Although there are constant revisions and changes to the algorithmic systems that govern the news feeds of social media platforms, there are several features that have essentially stayed consistent for a long time in virtually all of them. In this respect, I pay special attention to these devices' efforts to construct hierarchies among users, manifested, for example, by the privileges afforded to postings by verified profiles. It is thus critical to examine how far this kind of hierarchical structure of news feeds speaks to forms of recognition that embed an inherent inequality.

Before Elon Musk's purchase of the company in 2022, Twitter demanded that all verified accounts had to meet three basic criteria: they had to be *authentic* (i.e. belong to who they claim to); they had to be *active* (i.e. meet the platform's requirements for providing registered data and maintaining an active online presence within the past six months); and they had to be *notable* (i.e. belong to a prominent person or organization). This last criterion stands out since it required the individual or organization to have an active presence on data platforms such as Google Trends, Wikipedia and IMDB. It was also used as a criterion to verify if the 'account is detected to be in the top .05% follower or mention count for your geographic location'.[26] It is hard to know if the new subscription model for verified accounts on Twitter will be viable in the long term, but similarly to the traditional model, the subscription one is also based on the creation of hierarchies among users and incentives for them to be more active online.

Facebook equally imposes requirements for a profile to earn a 'verified badge'. The platform specifies four minimal, but not guaranteed, conditions for obtaining this privilege. The account needs to be authentic, unique, complete and notable. Notability is here described as representing 'a well-known, often searched person, brand or entity [online]'.[27]

Similar requirements for acquiring this sort of verification exist on other social media platforms. When considering personal profiles, which is the case in focus here, it is obvious that having a verified account necessitates the person's prior renown in many forms of media, especially in digital media that enable the quantification of this presence. In this respect, a consistent, active and notable presence on social media is a precondition for a person to strive to have their account verified and, as a result, achieve greater social recognition.

However, according to Couldry (2010), the establishment of more equitable societies necessarily involves the democratization of voice. This is not to say that Couldry embraces any form of voice, particularly those represented by what he refers to as 'tech populism'. For him, giving voice entails valuing social and human organizations that share genuine connections and uphold solidary values. These, nevertheless, are not the ideals that underpin the datafied logics of social media, which see human interactions as tools for increasing product sales (Thatcher et al., 2016; Couldry and Mejias, 2019b). The condition for a personal account on social media to be verified and, therefore, gain more power, does not necessarily include the representation of beliefs capable of constructing a more equal and democratic

The Demand for New Dispositions

society. For most platforms, what matters is the users' capacity to make themselves visible in the media, elicit reactions and stand out (Skeggs, 2014). And people are aware of these ideals. In her research on Instagram, Frier (2020, p. 231) states that 'everyone with a blue checkmark, after realizing that their comments would be prominently displayed, had an incentive to comment more'. Hearn similarly aims to understand how this type of logic alters people's personal dispositions. She proposes that 'free-lunch' incentives like the verification checkmarks, which vow to provide social recognition in the form of more reactions such as comments and 'likes', inspire 'users to perpetually work at posting and crafting themselves online' (Hearn, 2017, p. 73).

There are numerous necessary conditions for the subject to traverse social media platforms competently, especially if they want to acquire broad personal recognition in these spaces. First and foremost, they must always be connected and they must internalize the concept that a significant portion of their sociability must take place online. Of course, a permanent connection does not ensure the democratization of voices on social media. Ultimately, the platforms work according to the logic of quantifiable valuation, which necessitates a hierarchization capable of producing connections that match their economic demands. Even initiatives that encourage disconnection, colloquially known as a 'digital detox', frequently operate on the premise that people need to temporarily disconnect from social media in order to renew their energy and dispositions, allowing them to resume socializing on social media platforms at a later time (Kuntsman and Miyake, 2019).

The goal here is not to consider the potentially harmful psychological effects of the need to be constantly connected to social media. The development of a habitus linked to these datafied platforms, which offer social recognition to the individual, is considered here from the standpoint of its limits in the construction of citizenship. According to Honneth, struggles for recognition traditionally aim at fostering an individual's or social group's growth in self-confidence, self-respect and self-esteem. These struggles are also associated with broad changes that may lead to more egalitarian interactions between individuals. This recognition needs to be free and unconditional (Ikäheimo, 2015).

However, the pursuit of recognition via social media practices takes place in hierarchical contexts, where the production of an evaluative equality of subjects is an ideal at odds with the fundamental structures of the devices in question. According to Rieder et al. (2018), platforms like YouTube are constructed using algorithms that result in 'ranking cultures'. The authors define these cultures as 'unfolding processes of hierarchization and modulation of visibility that call on users, content creators and a platform that intervenes and circumscribes in various ways' (Rieder et al., 2018, p. 52). The authors were interested in knowing, for example, how to make ranking, as well as its pattern and structures, discernible to empirical study and how ranking manifests in relation to particular sociocultural concerns. The study they carried out using a methodology that enables viewing the results produced by YouTube's algorithm revealed, among other things, that the platform's search feature is particularly responsive to attention cycles. Within the scope of the study, the authors observed that the disproportionate presence of videos made by extremely active individuals with far-right ideological beliefs was favoured within the

The Demand for New Dispositions

hierarchy created by the YouTube algorithm. This was evident despite the fact that the videos at issue garnered fewer views than those reflecting more conciliatory and traditional viewpoints. In sum, Rieder et al. (2018, p. 64) observed that YouTube's ranking culture rewards content that seeks to express highly opinionated statements. This indicates how, within its hierarchical structure, this platform develops distinct emotional and psychological dispositions.

To summarize, datafied habitus can be understood as a set of behavioural, psychological and affective dispositions that guide an individual's practices and actions in social media. It is characterized by a drive to be always connected and active on these platforms. When followed, this drive is rewarded by the platform algorithms with higher visibility and status for the user in the news feeds. Furthermore, these psychological dispositions reveal a reflexive and self-objectified individual, who longs for self-representation online. Datafied habitus also refers to the spirit of cultivating relationships, friendships and followers on social media as a way of accruing material and symbolic benefits. In this sense, it represents a sociability geared not to the development of a sense of solidarity towards the other, but rather to an individualistic sense of civic worth.

The modulation of emotions within these dispositions is frequently aligned with strategies aimed at producing reactions from friends and followers on social media. These strategies include, for instance, the development of an 'authentic persona', built on opinionated statements, open displays of emotions and the exhibition of choices and tastes deemed as being original. They also encompass the administration of intimacy, the adoption of more informal modes towards the other, and a managed effort to blur dividing social differences and hierarchies. These dispositions were slowly cemented by historical social and economic transformations succeeded by the more recent development of visibility regimes of datafied platforms.

A weaker form of recognition

As seen in the examples provided in chapter 2, discussions about processes of mediated recognition are frequently based on the analysis of group practices or particular contexts, which makes it difficult to form a comprehensive understanding of ongoing processes of social transformation brought on by the spread of datafied social devices in everyday sociabilities. Even if social groups, such as the adolescents surveyed by Balleys et al. (2020), engage in forms of socialization on platforms such as YouTube in order to recognize themselves in others while also being recognized by their peers, we are unable to fully understand what YouTube means for these young people's identity formation processes. Balleys et al. observe how the young YouTubers' dialogical framework encourages the development of a sense of intimacy between the parties, which modulates the exchanges of messages, comments and 'likes', while structuring the recognition processes that the authors describe. These practices of commenting, liking and so on, when framed within the concept of 'expressive gestures of recognition', also characterized as 'allegories of a moral action' by Honneth and Margalit (2001), may therefore be described as a kind of *weak recognition*. This term refers to the datafied forms of recognition stated throughout this book that function as symbolic abbreviations and that include both the cognitive identification of a subject's existence and the assertion that this existence is acknowledged and validated by the other.

When reflecting on the pre-linguistic interactions between children and adults, Honneth and Margalit address the expressive gestures of recognition, such as smiling, nodding, etc., present in the early stages of an individual's existence. Naturally, this kind of recognition also happens in interactions involving just adults, throughout the innumerable routine practices of cognition and validation of the other that take place, for instance, when we nod our heads as we pass someone who is cleaning or repairing a public road. In this last instance, the recognition process is associated with the dimension of social esteem. In other words, by nodding to the person working on a public road, the subject makes it clear that the worker is both visible and engaged in a meritorious task. However, nothing ensures that the worker in question has complete access to the many aspects of citizenship required for him or her to be recognized as a subject, regardless of how many times during the day this kind of expression of recognition happens. In this regard, I contend that these expressive gestures of recognition that we give and receive every day, while necessary for the subject to feel valued and visible in daily circumstances, result in weak recognition because they do not increase the forms of freedom and equality required for the subject to achieve self-realization.

Similarly, the dynamics of datafied recognition explored by Balleys et al. (2020) and Lorenzana (2016), which occur via the usage of social plug-ins on digital platforms, produce visibility in addition to forms of self-validation and feelings of intimacy. Even while these sociability practices may raise participants' self-esteem in the particular setting of these interactions, in other circumstances they seem to function like an 'emotional seesaw', oscillating between having negative and positive impacts on individuals (Weinstein, 2018). Regardless of the dynamics analysed in each case, one should not lose sight of the platforms' differentiating and hierarchizing nature, as well as their datafied economic logics that displace the subject from their solidary relationship with the other in favour of a process of reflexive self-observation and self-objectification (Illouz, 2011).

Recognition in the age of social media platforms

It is possible to observe, therefore, a complex phenomenon regarding contemporary struggles for recognition. First, one can see a burgeoning economic and political transformation in recent decades, which is responsible for the expansion of the requirements needed for the individual to be fully recognized by society. As Souza (2003) and Boltanski and Chiapello (2009) suggest, the demands to be recognized as a full citizen who experiences a shared sense of universal dignity become increasingly challenging and difficult to fulfil. Today's connectionist world requires the development of dispositions linked to adaptability, flexibility and the acquisition of an entrepreneurial spirit, within a context that produces permanent vulnerability and individual competition. In this way, the quest for individual self-realization is becoming more coupled with feelings of anxiety and powerlessness.

The Demand for New Dispositions

At the same time, the issue of mass media and their relation to social processes and the formation of citizenship and recognition offers a distinct viewpoint. The contribution of the field of media and communication to this topic, which is often neglected or even left out of debates of political sociology, was highlighted primarily in chapter 2 of this book. Cottle (2007), Maia (2014) and Malik (2014), to name but a few, have conducted studies that illustrate the relevance of unbiased representation on mass media, like television, as a means of supporting groups fighting for recognition and social justice. In certain circumstances, large media corporations' decisions concerning the production and circulation of social representations are disputed and subsequently negotiated by minority groups who challenge failures of recognition by media companies (Maia, 2014). In general, scholars examining mediated recognition processes consider television, newspapers, and even social media as encouraging spaces of deliberation that, in most instances, have played a constructive role in shaping subjectivities capable of self-realization. As one would anticipate, this is especially true for public broadcasting services and alternative media controlled by indigenous and minority groups (Couldry, 2012; Malik, 2014).

The discussion of the recent emergence, maybe over the last decade or so, of a form of 'attitudinal mindset' – or set of dispositions – associated with social media is the third phenomenon this book examines. It is integrally connected to the previous two and is a key focus point in the book. If the mass media provide fertile ground for struggles over recognition for disfranchised groups, social media offer an unprecedented capacity for the subject's self-representation, allowing actors greater agency in the search for valuative transformations in society and expanding their status as citizens in many situations. This capacity does come at a price, though. The quest for self-representation and recognition on platforms such as Facebook, Instagram and Twitter takes place in settings regulated by datafied structures that reward particular regimes of emotion and self-regulation while requiring the subject's constant connection. This context, I argue, favours the development of behavioural dispositions that combine the subject's growing demand for flexibility, adaptation and entrepreneurship with a continuous effort to internalize the metrical logic that runs through social media and ultimately strives to bring the platforms economic advantages. Historically, media visibility regimes have always been connected to celebrities and entertainment idols. However, more lately, a dissemination of what I have termed the datafied habitus has been noticed. That is, we have seen the rise of manuals, courses, tutorials, and even an algorithmic imaginary, that seek to intervene in the dispositions needed to amplify the recognition of an individual's value in data-driven social media.

Yet, unlike emancipatory struggles for recognition, which traditionally have as their core objective the consolidation of underprivileged groups' right to equality and freedom, the search for datafied recognition involves the individual adhering to a moral model that gives value to identities and practices linked to the world of social media (Lim, 2021). Even if expressive gestures of recognition can produce perceptions of self-esteem gain in social media, they occur in spaces that use hierarchical logics that frequently value feelings and opinions with a greater capacity to

The Demand for New Dispositions

create conflicts and strong emotional reactions, while also escalating precarious conditions. In sum, it is an individualized and commodified form of recognition that does not reinforce a communal sense of solidarity and freedom.

Conclusion

The idea that social media both influence and are influenced by contemporary forms of self-representation and sociability, as discussed throughout this book, is not novel. There is a considerable body of literature exploring, for instance, the establishment of emotional expression norms on Facebook, Instagram and similar platforms (Qiu et al., 2012; Waterloo et al., 2018), the impact of social media on affective relationships and friendships (Baym, 2010; Gershon, 2011; David and Cambre, 2016; Vriens and Van Ingen, 2018; Standlee, 2019), as well as research on self-representation in this type of media (Illouz, 2011; Thumim, 2012).

Similarly, numerous thought-provoking studies have investigated the relationship between digital social media and the spread of neoliberal logics in shaping current subjectivities. Often, this phenomenon is characterized by analysing the media practices of profiles known as digital influencers. According to Abidin, influencers are:

> everyday, ordinary Internet users who accumulate a relatively large following on blogs and social media

Conclusion

through the textual and visual narration of their personal lives and lifestyles, engage with their following in digital and physical spaces, and monetise their following by integrating 'advertorials' into their blog or social media posts. (Abidin, 2015, p. 1)

Discussions of the phenomenon of influencers, and related variants like lifestyle gurus (Baker and Rojek, 2020), creators (Arriagada and Ibáñez, 2020) and YouTubers (Burgess and Green, 2009), typically centre on the articulation between personal exposure, high visibility on social media and the ability to gain financial advantages for the individual in question. This ideal of the subject has become prevalent to the point that it is now commonly embraced by teenagers (Jorge et al., 2018; Balleys et al., 2020), children (Tomaz, 2019), parents of infants (Johnson, 2014; Holiday et al., 2020; Jorge et al., 2022), and even pet owners, as depicted by Frier (2020 p. 141) in her account of the first successful influencers on Instagram. However, it is argued here that certain underlying features that constitute this model of the neoliberal subject, who seeks to monetize their presence on social media, are extensively present among ordinary users of these platforms too. These characteristics form a specific primary habitus, which I refer to as datafied habitus.

The emotional and psychological dispositions inherent in this primary habitus are increasingly influenced by the incorporation and naturalization of new algorithmic imaginaries, as outlined by Schulz (2023). These encompass, according to the author, the expectations created by the algorithmic processes themselves and their creators, as well as the users' perspectives. Primary habitus is a concept that includes, among other things, the relationship between individuals and their emotional and affective expressions with what Foucault refers to as the technologies of the self. Hence, some of the arguments presented throughout this book regarding the relationship between neoliberal subjectivities and social media correspond to works by Marwick (2013), Biressi (2017), Abidin (2018), Scolere et al. (2018), Duffy and Pooley (2019) and Glatt (2022), among others.

The perspective presented here not only reinforces but also complements the endeavours made by the authors mentioned above, as it originates from a distinct standpoint. While there are numerous valuable contributions regarding the topic, Marwick's book, considered one of the most influential works in delineating this relationship, provides a suitable foundation for advancing this argument. Through dozens of interviews and extensive fieldwork in the San Francisco region of California, Marwick investigates how the technology start-up scene in that region reproduces contemporary capitalism's principles. According to the author, social media developed in that part of the world are imbued with logics that assist individuals in self-governing, thus aligning with the tenets of market neoliberalism. Additionally, the structuring principles of these technologies are directly influenced by the socioeconomic context in which they were created. Marwick refers to the context of the venture-backed start-up scene, which incorporates ideals of the myth of meritocracy, individual entrepreneurship, corporate deregulation and labour market flexibility. In other words, the researcher proposes that technologies such as social media not only are products of but also further perpetuate market capitalism.

Her analysis identifies key elements like the development of techniques such as lifestreaming and self-branding that amplify participants' status in the

Conclusion

researched scene. Status refers to someone's situation, emotional state, or opinion about something, but, primarily for the case at hand, it also refers to a subject's relative social position, that is, a classification in relation to others. In this sense, the constant pursuit of status is connected to the creation and maintenance of inequality between people. It means prioritizing the effort for attention and visibility, which are increasingly contested and scarce resources today. Marwick focuses on how self-branding ideals, such as authenticity, meritocracy and entrepreneurship, are used to rationalize discriminatory practices that, for instance, prevent women reaching top positions in the technology industry. Her work reveals how the technology scene in the San Francisco region and the Web 2.0 technologies it created are significant contemporary forces in the production of digital elitism that justifies enormous social, gender and racial inequalities.

The discussions by Marwick and other authors who explore the constitution of neoliberal subjectivities in digital media directly intersect with the concept of datafied habitus discussed throughout this book. Yet, I believe that the concept of habitus, particularly from Souza's perspective, can offer a more comprehensive viewpoint on the impact of digital media on the struggles for recognition and citizenship. This perspective may provide a deeper understanding than the notion of the tech scene's ideology.

Recognition, citizenship and the media

As previously discussed in this book, habitus is a key concept for Bourdieu in his sociological theory of practice. It refers to the dispositions, attitudes, values and tastes that are formed through an individual's experiences and socialization within a particular cultural and historical context. Bourdieu emphasizes the importance of the habitus in shaping cultural production, including artistic and literary forms, and in determining what is deemed aesthetically valuable and legitimate. In contrast, Souza approaches the concept through the competencies required for an individual to be regarded as a complete and dignified citizen. That is to say, the Brazilian sociologist proposes to consider habitus not in terms of the formation of taste or the consumption of material and symbolic goods, but rather through the creation of competencies that enable the individual and their achievements to be recognized as having value. Souza labels this set of dispositions the primary habitus, while Bourdieu's concept is referred to as the secondary habitus. This differentiation helps to clarify how the habitus concept is connected to the idea of recognition.

Although Souza's study was originally designed to analyse the origins of social inequalities in the Global South, the emotional, affective and psychological competencies that enable individuals to be recognized universally as dignified and valuable persons are also, as understood here, connected to their relationship with social media. However, to distinguish these competencies from what Souza generically refers to as primary habitus or, in his more recent works (2012, 2018), characterizes as the dispositions of hard workers, we propose the concept of datafied habitus. The use of the idea of datafication to think about these new dispositions is crucial, since both social plug-ins that operate as attributors of value to online practices and news feeds that, so to speak, 'distribute the sensible', are

Conclusion

structured in quantitative logics. That is, the individual's relationship with themselves and with the other currently involves algorithmic processes of tabulation and metricized analysis. In the era of 'datafied citizens', as Barassi (2019) notes, we are all coerced into participating in digital platforms. If social media posts are not viewed, liked or commented on positively, people question their own value. Consequently, the use of social media can be seen both as a form of self-entrepreneurship for individuals seeking to achieve economic and symbolic benefits on digital platforms, as argued by Marwick (2013), Scolere et al. (2018) and others, and as a means of inserting themselves into sociability dynamics necessary for their formation as citizens.

As discussed earlier in this book, the connection between citizenship and media is well established in the field of communication studies. Yet, this articulation takes on different forms depending on the context in which it is used. One of the most common is that which sees the media as having a decisive role in shaping a cultural citizenship. In this view, the media are crucial for the different social groups constituting a community to express their values and individualities. That is, the media are considered privileged spaces of social deliberation and representation, spaces that are potentially producers of media recognition (Maia, 2014). Cultural citizenship, according to Pakulski (1997), becomes particularly relevant today when traditional dimensions that ensure civic worth, such as social welfare, are losing ground. Fenton (2009) and Turner (2010), however, argue that although discourse on citizenship and participation may have become more prevalent in entertainment programmes, such as television shows, they are less enacted in practice.

Recognition in the Age of Social Media

The formation of new types of citizenship through specific television genres, such as reality shows, has been analysed by some authors, such as Ouellette and Hay (2008) and Biressi and Nunn (2014). Weber (2009), for instance, focuses on makeover TV shows and how they create an imagined community of belonging based on shared values of autonomy, class mobility, egalitarianism and self-making. However, this imagined community is exclusionary, as certain groups or individuals are inevitably left outside. The process of affective domination used in makeover shows disciplines subjects into citizenship through shaming and love-power. Citizenship status is often restricted and reinforces exclusion, while claims for inclusion demand compliance with normalizing criteria. Shows like *The Great American Makeover*, a case in point, champion access to restricted privileges, while supporting the ideology of free-market meritocracy. For Weber, this type of show engages in a project of citizenship marked by 'neoliberal ideologies, which position the subject as an entrepreneur of the self, who does and, indeed, must engage in care of the body' (Weber, 2009, p. 39). The benefits of citizenship are applied unequally, particularly for groups who are marginalized because of their gender, sexuality, race, ethnicity and class.

Recent studies that explore the relationship between data-driven platforms and new forms of citizenship highlight the inequalities inherent in their structures. Barassi (2019) points out that individuals' personal data, defining their civil rights as public subjects, are increasingly being collected by these technologies, blurring the lines between consumer subject and citizen subject. Chambers (2017) is also concerned about the constant demands for connecting and sharing by social media.

Conclusion

She argues that these forms of sociability, characterized by algorithmic friendship and scalable relationships, have the potential to challenge traditional notions of citizenship by creating new forms of belonging and participation. However, she also notes that the engineered connectedness demanded by these platforms, which entails technical affordances, persistence and careful self-management, can be exclusionary and can reinforce existing power structures, thus limiting opportunities for participation and citizenship (ibid., p. 30).

Even Kuntsman (2017), who celebrates the possibility of new forms of citizenship emerging from media practices associated with social media, is concerned with the expansion of datafication processes that create an illusion of proximity and capitalize on the desire for individual visibility creation.

Platforms, algorithms and civic value

The discussions above share a common articulation between citizenship and social media that focuses on the individual's absorption of specific self-regulation and sociability modes of datafied technologies. In other words, instead of focusing on an idea of cultural citizenship, these perspectives connect with Souza's analyses that relate the constitution of individual civic value with the acquisition of certain psychological and emotional dispositions. The argument that I put forward here in this book is that these modes of self-regulation and sociability linked to social media are structured within a specific habitus that promotes the pursuit of a weak and individualized form of recognition, which does not necessarily produce greater equality and solidarity among individuals. In some cases, the creation of an individual sense of civic worth on social media occurs within practices of disrespect and aggression, highlighting some of the limits of the search for recognition on datafied platforms.

In a certain sense, this is one of the findings of Magalhães' (2019) research on the use of Facebook by Brazilians during the political crisis experienced in the country between 2013 and 2018. Magalhães' work analyses the processes of civic becoming of ordinary Brazilians, in the light of their use of Facebook, the most popular social media platform in the country. Through empirical research based on dozens of interviews, the author seeks to understand how the datafication processes of the platform engineered patterns of seeing and reading that influenced their actions and self-perception as citizens. Participants' understanding of citizenship and democracy in Brazil, combined with their imaginary of Facebook's algorithmic visibility system, resulted in a paradoxical notion of how to have a voice on the platform. This notion led to a unique civic imaginary that revolves around controlling one's visibility by silencing oneself and others. Magalhães refers to this phenomenon as 'bottom-up authoritarianism', in which ordinary users undermine their own civic autonomy through their actions. This insight highlights the connection between civic autonomy and datafication, and how Facebook's datafication practices indirectly shape the user's civic voice. In sum, the author found that

> To be seen (and likely heard) by their peers, many interviewees considered hateful, simplified and manipulative civic voice expressions to be necessary. They seemed

Conclusion

to infer that if Facebook's news feed privileges posts and comments that receive large amounts of datafied reactions, any expression that can entice others into reacting is understood as itself enticing. *Disrespect for others appeared as an unavoidable consequence of the interviewee's own attempts to be respected.* (ibid., p. 228, my italics)

These findings not only reinforce the idea that Facebook's news feed amplifies the circulation of voices capable of generating the most user reactions, which often happens with opinionated posts or those that provoke strong emotions, as argued by Rieder et al. (2018), but also that individuals take this belief into account when constructing their own self-perception. One participant in Magalhães' research stated that when one of his posts does not receive at least fifty 'likes', he deletes it, as he believes that 'what I have published ... *might not be exactly what I think* [emphasis added]' (Magalhães, 2019, p. 215). Put differently, this participant's self-perception is directly dependent on how people react to his expressions on social media. For him, if people don't 'like' or share one of his publications, it means that the publication doesn't reflect what he is (or what he thinks). In another circumstance, a different participant in the study revealed that by invisibilizing elements of himself that might get the wrong type of attention because of how the news feed operates, he believed he had discovered which civic voice better reflected his persona. The examples above illustrate what Magalhães calls the *prefiguration cycle of civic voice*.

Although Magalhães' research is situated within the political transformations occurring in Brazil in the 2010s, which are not the focus of this book, it provides valuable insights into the influence of the datafied logics of social media, and the imaginary surrounding them, and into the emotional and psychological self-regulation of their users, as well as the development of the perception of recognition and civic value of these subjects.

In this context, I would like to emphasize another aspect of Magalhães' research that I believe is closely related to a fundamental underlying issue present in Souza's work. I mention this issue here in the book's conclusion as it is relevant and has potential for further research. Specifically, I am referring to how the sociocultural context can influence the development and adaptation of individuals to a primary habitus associated with data-driven social media, as they struggle for recognition.

Souza's work is primarily focused on exploring the emergence of sub-citizenship in Brazil, in the Global South in general, and increasingly in marginalized groups in the Global North. As seen in previous chapters, this issue is analysed through the behavioural dispositions necessary for individuals and social groups to gain access to a more basic form of social recognition. When absent, these dispositions lead, according to discussions in Boltanski (1999), Boltanski and Chiapello (2009) and Souza (2003, 2011), to a type of symbolic and material exclusion of individuals in society. In his latest work, Souza (2012) advances this debate by describing the spread of emotional and psychological modes of regulation that are characteristic of a struggling class aspiring to social mobility. However, these modes point to a subordinate inclusion that reflects the current precariousness of social and work relations. The significance of this debate lies in its ability to highlight the importance of an individual's

Conclusion

socioeconomic context in the development, or not, of specific types of habitus linked to subjects' autonomy and dignity.

Magalhães' work is pertinent to this discussion as he proposes the existence of a relationship between the socioeconomic context of the participants in his research and their perception of the possibility of constructing a civic voice in Facebook's news feed. The author uses the concept of *sociomateriality* to suggest that interviewees' perceptions of which individuals are visible on the platform are influenced by their broader understanding of the societal rules that dictate whose civic voice is considered valuable in a country characterized by deep-rooted inequalities, authoritarianism and elitism. This hybridization of assumptions and relational understandings shapes interviewees' perspectives on the platform's visibility norms. Magalhães (2019, p. 230) asserts that '[b]eing a woman, transgender, Black, a man, White, affluent appeared in the descriptions of some of the interviewees as a critical factor to how they imagined specific others and, thus, to their expected recognitions and misrecognitions within Facebook'.

Magalhães' research highlights the impact of Facebook users' socioeconomic and identity characteristics on how their voices are recognized, projected and perceived by the platform and others. This demonstrates that datafied platforms, and the associated imaginaries built around them, can significantly alter the recognition processes that shape individuals' everyday lives.

Based on these issues, I believe it is legitimate to speculate whether there is a correlation between the effort by a segment of society to seek recognition on datafied social media platforms, on the one hand, and the lack of access to different forms of citizenship, on the other. In other words, the discussions above prompt me to conjecture whether the lack of experience of basic, universalized principles of citizenship contributes to the transformation of the search for datafied recognition into a sort of 'fast track' towards a sense of inclusion that is supposedly able to provide self-esteem and self-respect. Empirical research indicates that the use of social media platforms varies depending on the demographic group and the region of the world being analysed. However, there is a quantitative pattern, observed for many years, that concerns the level of engagement in these technologies by populations from different countries. According to the Data Overview Report,[28] nine of the top ten countries with the highest average number of social media platforms used per user through 2022 are low- or middle-income countries (the United Arab Emirates is the only high-income country in this group). Perhaps even more intriguing is the finding that all ten countries with the highest average daily time spent on social media per capita are low- or middle-income countries, despite having lower internet penetration relative to high-income countries. The report lists Nigeria in first place, with an average daily social media usage of 4 hours and 36 minutes, followed by Brazil, South Africa, the Philippines and Kenya, just to name the top five on the list.

The reasons for these statistics are many, and I do not seek to offer any simplistic explanation for the phenomenon in this conclusion. However, I believe that the possibility of articulating the existence of different degrees of sociability on social media with the search for contemporary forms of recognition on these platforms, especially in groups experiencing lack of recognition or misrecognition, is promising.

Conclusion

Final remarks

This discussion is aligned with the general objective of this book, which is to draw attention to how recognition processes are changing in the context of contemporary social media platforms. In the first chapters, I argue that struggles for recognition are essential to forming a just society, in which citizens are treated as equals in their rights and are free to assert their singularities to reach their full potential. Drawing on existing scholarship, I examine and problematize how social media reproduce and construct contemporary social life. Although social media platforms differ from each other in many ways, they share a common feature: news feeds, which curate and value individuals' expressions and self-representations. This algorithmic process continuously ranks users' actions and connections, prioritizing behaviours and affects that generate greater engagement, even if this can sometimes result in commodification or radicalization. To contextualize these changes, I provide a brief analysis of the historical transformations in regimes of behavioural and emotional self-regulation of western subjects, from Erasmus of Rotterdam in the sixteenth century to the present day. This effort aims to highlight changes in power relations present in practices of sociability and self-representation that are contemporarily mediated by datafication processes. Ultimately, this discussion deepens the debate on the dispositions required for the subject to feel fully recognized as a citizen in the context of social media. This argument explores how recent changes in capitalism intersect with the demand for a datafied habitus, which, as I propose ultimately, results in individuals conforming to moral models that use social media for personal gain.

Recognition in the Age of Social Media

As argued by Honneth, struggles for recognition have been playing, throughout history, a crucial role in the processes of social transformation. Through these struggles, minority and marginalized groups have expanded their access to civil, political, social and cultural rights. Recognition in these spheres is crucial in both the individual and social dimensions, but it does not occur without a fight. In an age in which media play a significant part in people's relationship with the world, it is only natural to assume that media have become a fertile ground for such struggles. Social media, in particular, appear to have fulfilled the contemporary subject's basic need for recognition by offering, like no other type of media, a promise of democratization of social respect and esteem. However, this book argues that the recognition offered by these platforms primarily serves the economic interests of their corporations rather than promoting freedom and solidarity, which raises questions about the ideal of transformation towards a more just society that permeates the myths surrounding this type of technology.

Notes

1 According to the Digital 2023 Global Overview Report, published in partnership with We Are Social and Meltwater, internet users use an average of seven different social media platforms in any given month. This suggests that social media use is spread over several technologies. The 2023 report is available at https://datareportal.com/reports/digital-2023-global-overview-report (accessed 28 February 2023).
2 https://www.statista.com/statistics/433871/daily-social-media-usage-worldwide/ (accessed 24 November 2022).
3 It is worth noting that the concept of recognition is present in earlier works of Ricoeur, Berlin and others. However, it was only with Honneth and Taylor that it gained pre-eminence in debates on identity formation and social struggles.
4 Souza refers to these nations as peripheral societies.
5 As examples, Souza cites the English Poor Laws, the Great Awakenings, which took place during the eighteenth and nineteenth centuries in the United States, and other similar processes occurring in France.
6 When I speak of legal recognition I am not referring

only to the making of laws, but to the capacity of the legal system to carry them out. I adopt a perspective similar to Hegel's in which the mere description of laws is not enough to guarantee their application.
7 I am indebted to Nick Couldry for raising this point in a previous work.
8 Some of these perspectives were debated at two related academic events on the subject. The first was a thematic panel titled 'Mediated Recognition: Agency, Paradoxes, and Struggles for Visibility', which took place at the 2018 International Communication Association (ICA) conference held in Prague. The second event was the 2019 ICA pre-conference, 'Mediated Recognition: Identity, Justice, and Activism', held in Washington, DC.
9 Many works on recognition theory had been published before that, of course. Not only the already mentioned key works from Hegel, but also writings of Fichte and Kant in the eighteenth century, and the more recent work of Berlin, are good examples.
10 Italics in the original.
11 https://tech.facebook.com/engineering/2021/1/news-feed-ranking (accessed 24 November 2022).
12 https://quantifiedself.com (accessed 1 June 2023).
13 Originally proposed by Foucault, the concept of 'dispositive' was further developed by Agamben (2009) when discussing contemporary forms of dispersed power, as will be seen later in this book.
14 https://tech.fb.com/news-feed-ranking/ (accessed 1 June 2023).
15 https://www.rsph.org.uk/about-us/news/instagram-ranked-worst-for-young-people-s-mental-health.html (accessed 1 June 2023).
16 Vishal Shah's interview on the podcast *Geekout With Matt Navarra*. https://anchor.fm/geekoutmattnavarra/episodes/8--Instagrams-Vishal-Shah-ea7gns (accessed 1 June 2023).

Notes to pages 81–148

17 https://www.socialmediatoday.com/news/instagrams-vp-of-product-provides-insight-into-its-hidden-like-count-test/570610/ (accessed 1 June 2023).
18 It should be noted that in late 2022 Twitter introduced a paid form of verification, which made this process more open to users in general.
19 The original videos analysed here are not available online anymore. However, Nunes launched an updated version of the course in 2022, which is available at https://cursoswhindersson.com.br/como-ser-interessante/ (accessed 24 November 2022).
20 https://about.youtube (accessed 1 June 2023).
21 https://www.youtube.com/watch?v=hPxnIix5ExI (accessed 1 June 2023).
22 My italics.
23 My italics.
24 https://www.forbes.com/sites/johnkoetsier/2021/12/27/top-10-most-downloaded-apps-and-games-of-2021-tiktok-telegram-big-winners (accessed 24 November 2022).
25 https://www.statista.com/statistics/433871/daily-social-media-usage-worldwide/ (accessed 20 November 2022).
26 https://help.twitter.com/en/managing-your-account/about-twitter-verified-accounts (accessed 24 November 2022).
27 https://www.facebook.com/help/1288173394636262 (accessed 24 November 2022).
28 The Data Overview Report is published in partnership with We Are Social and Meltwater. The 2023 report is available at https://datareportal.com/reports/digital-2023-global-overview-report (accessed 28 February 2023).

References

Abidin, C. (2015). Communicative <3 intimacies: influencers and perceived interconnectedness. *Ada: A Journal of Gender, New Media, & Technology*, 8. Retrieved from https://scholarsbank.uoregon.edu/xmlui/bitstream/handle/1794/26365/ada08-commu-abi-2015.pdf?sequence=1&isAllowed=y/ (accessed 17 July 2023)

Abidin, C. (2018). *Internet celebrity: Understanding fame online*. Bingley: Emerald Publishing.

Agamben, G. (2009). *O que é o contemporâneo? e outros ensaios*. Chapecó: Argos.

Ajana, B. (2018). Introduction. In: Ajana, B. (ed.) *Self-tracking: Empirical and philosophical investigations* (pp. 1–10). Basingstoke: Palgrave Macmillan.

Andacht, F. (2003). Uma aproximação analítica do formato televisual do reality show Big Brother. *Galáxia*, 6, 145–64.

Andersen, J. (2018). Archiving, ordering, and searching: search engines, algorithms, databases, and deep mediatization. *Media, Culture & Society*, 40(8), 1135–50. https://doi.org/10.1177/0163443718754652

Ang, I. (1985). *Watching Dallas*. London: Methuen.

Araújo, W. (2018). A construção da norma algorítmica: análise dos textos sobre o Feed de Notícias do Facebook.

References

E-Compós (Brasília), 21(1). https://doi.org/10.30962/ec.v21i1.1402

Araújo, W. (2021). Norma algorítmica como técnica de governo em plataformas digitais: um estudo da Escola de Criadores de Conteúdo do YouTube. *Revista Fronteiras*, 23(1), 29–39. https://doi.org/10.4013/fem.2021.231.03

Araújo, W., & Magalhães, J. C. (2018). Eu, eu mesmo e o algoritmo: como usuários do Twitter falam sobre o 'algoritmo' para performar a si mesmos. *Proceedings of the 27th annual Compós conference*, pp. 1–22.

Arriagada, A., & Ibáñez, F. (2020). 'You need at least one picture daily, if not, you're dead': content creators and platform evolution in the social media ecology. *Social Media + Society*, 6(3). https://doi.org/10.1177/2056305120944624

Aufderheide, P. (ed.) (1993). *Media literacy: A report of the national leadership conference on media literacy*. Aspen, CO: Aspen Institute.

Baker, S., & Rojek, C. (2020). *Lifestyle gurus: Constructing authority and influence online*. Cambridge: Polity.

Balleys, C., Millerand, F., Thoër, C., & Duque, N. (2020). Searching for oneself on YouTube: teenage peer socialization and social recognition processes. *Social Media + Society*, 6(2). https://doi.org/10.1177/2056305120909474

Banet-Weiser, S. (2015). Keynote address: Media, markets, gender: economies of visibility in a neoliberal moment. *The Communication Review*, 18(1), 53–70. https://doi.org/10.1080/10714421.2015.996398

Barakat, C. (2014). Science links selfies to narcissism, addiction and low self-esteem. *SocialTimes*. Retrieved from https://www.adweek.com/performance-marketing/selfies-narcissism-addiction-low-self-esteem/ (accessed 1 June 2023)

References

Barassi, V. (2019). Datafied citizens in the age of coerced digital participation. *Sociological Research Online*, 24(3), 414–29. https://doi.org/10.1177/1360780419857734

Bargas, J., & Maia, R. (2017). Quilombolas no WhatsApp: o papel do aprendizado coletivo nas lutas por reconhecimento. *Comunicação Mídia e Consumo*, 14(41), 31–52.

Barthes, R. (1973). *Mythologies*. London: Paladin.

Baym, N. K. (2010). *Personal connections in the digital age*. Cambridge: Polity.

Baym, N. K. (2018). *Playing to the crowd: Musicians, audiences, and the intimate work of connection*. New York: NYU Press.

Bell, C. (1992). *Ritual theory, ritual practice*. New York: Oxford University Press.

Bell, C. (2009). *Ritual: Perspectives and dimensions*. New York: Oxford University Press.

Berger, P. (1983). On the obsolescence of the concept of honor. In: Hauerwas, S., & MacIntyre, A. (eds.) *Revisions: Changing perspectives in moral philosophy* (pp. 172–81). Notre Dame, IN: University of Notre Dame Press.

Berger, P., & Luckmann, T. (1966). *The social construction of reality*. London: Penguin.

Bhandari, A., & Bimo, S. (2022). Why's everyone on TikTok now? The algorithmized self and the future of self-making on social media. *Social Media + Society*, 8(1). https://doi.org/10.1177/20563051221086241

Biressi, A. (2017). Idols of self-production: selfies, career success, and social class. In: Deery, J., & Press, A. (eds.) *Media and class: TV, film and digital culture* (pp. 131–45). New York: Routledge.

Biressi, A., & Nunn, H. (2014). 'I'm passionate, Lord Sugar': young entrepreneurs, critical judgment, and emotional labor in Young Apprentice. In: Panse, S.,

References

& Rothermel, D. (eds.) *Critique of judgment in film and television* (pp. 90–107). Basingstoke: Palgrave Macmillan.

Bishop, S. (2018). Anxiety, panic and self-optimization: inequalities and the YouTube algorithm. *Convergence*, 24(1), 69–84. https://doi.org/10.1177/1354856517736978

Bishop, S. (2020). Algorithmic experts: selling algorithmic lore on YouTube. *Social Media + Society*, 6(1). https://doi.org/10.1177/2056305119897323

Boltanski, L. (1999). *Distant suffering: Morality, media and politics*. Cambridge: Cambridge University Press.

Boltanski, L., & Chiapello, È. (2009). *O novo espírito do capitalismo*. São Paulo: Martins Fontes.

Borges, G., Sigiliano, D., & Guida, V. (2021). Competência midiática e formação para a cidadania: oficinas de criação do Observatório da Qualidade no Audiovisual. *Tríade: Comunicação, Cultura e Mídia*, 9(20), 24–50. https://doi.org/10.22484/2318-5694.2021v9n20p24-50

Bourdieu, P. (1979). *Algeria: Essays*. Cambridge: Cambridge University Press.

Bourdieu, P. (1986). The forms of capital. In: Richardson, J. G. (ed.) *Handbook of theory and research for the sociology of education* (pp. 241–58). Westport, CT: Greenwood.

Bourdieu, P. (1990). *Language and symbolic power*. Cambridge: Polity.

Bourdieu, P. (2000). *Distinction: A social critique of the judgement of taste*. London: Routledge.

Bourdieu, P. (2002). Habitus. In: Hillier, J., & Rooksby, E. (eds.) *Habitus: A sense of place* (pp. 43–9). Burlington, VT: Ashgate.

Braudy, L. (1986). *The frenzy of renown: Fame and its history*. Oxford: Oxford University Press.

Brunsdon, C. (1995). The role of soap opera in the development of feminist television scholarship. In: Allen,

References

R. C. (ed.) *To be continued ...: Soap operas around the world* (pp. 49–65). London: Routledge.

Bucher, T. (2017). The algorithmic imaginary: exploring the ordinary affects of Facebook algorithms. *Information, Communication & Society*, 20(1), 30–44. https://doi.org/10.1080/1369118X.2016.1154086

Bucher, T. (2018). *If ... then: Algorithmic power and politics*. Oxford: Oxford University Press.

Buckingham, D. (2007). Digital media literacies: rethinking media education in the age of the internet. *Research in Comparative and International Education*, 2(1), 43–55. https://doi.org/10.2304/rcie.2007.2.1.43

Burgess, J., & Green, J. (2009). *YouTube: Online video and participatory culture*. Cambridge: Polity.

Burke, P. (1994). *A fabricação do rei: a construção da imagem pública de Luiz XIV*. Rio de Janeiro: Zahar Editora.

Campanella, B. (2012). *Os olhos do grande irmão: uma etnografia dos fãs do Big Brother Brasil*. Porto Alegre: Sulina.

Campanella, B. (2013). Tirando as máscaras: o reality show e a busca pela autenticidade no mundo contemporâneo. *E-Compós* (Brasília), 16(1), 1–17. https://doi.org/10.30962/ec.872

Campanella, B. (2014). Novas práticas, antigos rituais: a organização do cotidiano e as configurações de poder na mídia. *Revista GEMInIS*, S. l., 8–12.

Campanella, B. (2020). Celebrity activism and the making of solidarity capital. In: Farrel, N. (ed.) *The political economy of celebrity activism* (pp. 19–34). New York: Routledge.

Campanella, B., Nantes, J., & Fernandes, P. (2018). Criando intimidade, recebendo visibilidade: novas práticas de persuasão na economia da fama. *Comunicação, Mídia e Consumo* (São Paulo), 15(43), 158–77. https://doi.org/10.18568/CMC.V15I43.1474

References

Chambers, D. (2017). Networked intimacy: algorithmic friendship and scalable sociality. *European Journal of Communication*, 32(1), 26–36. https://doi.org/10.1177/0267323116682792

Chouliaraki, L. (2013). *The ironic spectator: Solidarity in the age of post-humanitarianism*. Malden, MA and Cambridge: Polity.

Christl, W., & Spiekermann, S. (2016). *Networks of control: A report on corporate surveillance, digital tracking, big data and privacy*. Vienna: Facultas.

Cottle, S. (2007). Mediatized recognition and the 'other'. *Media International Australia*, 123, 34–48.

Couldry, N. (2002). Playing for celebrity: Big Brother as ritual event. *Television & New Media*, 3(3), 283–93. https://doi.org/10.1177/152747640200300304

Couldry, N. (2003a). Media meta-capital: extending the range of Bourdieu's field theory. *Theory and Society*, 32(5–6), 653–77. https://doi.org/10.1007/1-4020-2589-0_8

Couldry, N. (2003b). *Media rituals: A critical approach*. Abingdon: Routledge.

Couldry, N. (2005). Media rituals: beyond functionalism. In: Rothenbuhler, E. W., & Coman, M. (eds.) *Media anthropology* (pp. 59–69). Thousand Oaks, CA: Sage.

Couldry, N. (2010). *Why voice matters: Culture and politics after neoliberalism*. London: Sage.

Couldry, N. (2012). *Media, society, world: Social theory and digital media practice*. Cambridge: Polity.

Couldry, N. (2015). The myth of 'us': digital networks, political change and the production of collectivity. *Information, Communication & Society*, 18(6), 608–26. https://doi.org/10.1080/1369118X.2014.979216

Couldry, N., & Hepp, A. (2017). *The mediated construction of reality*. Cambridge: Polity.

Couldry, N., & Mejias, U. (2019a). Data colonialism:

References

rethinking big data's relation to the contemporary subject. *Television & New Media*, 20(4), 336–49. https://doi.org/10.1177/1527476418796632

Couldry, N., & Mejias, U. (2019b). *The costs of connection: How data is colonizing human life and appropriating it for capitalism*. Stanford, CA: Stanford University Press.

David, G., & Cambre, C. (2016). Screened intimacies: Tinder and the swipe logic. *Social Media + Society*, 2(2). https://doi.org/10.1177/2056305116641976

Davies, W. (2021). The politics of recognition in the age of social media. *New Left Review*, 128, March/April.

De Oliveira, C., & Nunes, M. (2011). *Cidadania e cultura digital*. Rio de Janeiro: e-Papers.

De Vito, M. A. (2016). From editors to algorithms. *Digital Journalism*, 5(6), 753–73. https://doi.org/10.1080/21670811.2016.1178592

Deller, R. (2015). Religion as makeover: reality, lifestyle and spiritual transformation. *International Journal of Cultural Studies*, 18(3), 291–303. https://doi.org/10.1177/1367877913513687

Desmurget, M. (2019). *A fábrica de cretinos digitais*. São Paulo: Vestígio.

Dodge, M., & Kitchin, R. (2001). *Mapping cyberspace*. London: Routledge.

Douglas, M. (1984). *Purity and danger*. London: Ark Paperbacks.

Driessens, O. (2013). Celebrity capital: redefining celebrity using field theory. *Theory and Society*, 42, 543–60. https://doi.org/10.1007/s11186-013-9202-3

Duarte, L. F. (1986). *Da vida nervosa nas classes trabalhadoras urbanas*. Rio de Janeiro: Jorge Zahar Editor.

Duffy, B. E., & Pooley, J. (2019). Idols of promotion: the triumph of self-branding in an age of precarity. *Journal of Communication*, 69(1), 26–48. https://doi.org/10.1093/joc/jqy063

References

Durkheim, E. (1995). *The elementary forms of religious life*. Translated by K. Fields. New York: Free Press.

Dyer, R. (1998). *Stars*. London: British Film Institute.

Edwards, L. (2018). Public relations, voice and recognition: a case study. *Media, Culture & Society*, 40(3), 317–32. https://doi.org/10.1177/0163443717705000

Elias, N. (1978). *What is sociology?* London: Hutchinson.

Elias, N. (2000). *The civilizing process: Sociogenetic and psychogenetic investigations*. Oxford: Blackwell Publishers.

Faimau, G. (2013). *Socio-cultural construction of recognition: The discursive representation of Islam and Muslims in the British Christian news media*. Newcastle upon Tyne: Cambridge Scholars Publishing.

Feldman, L. (2004). *Citizens without shelter: Homelessness, democracy, and political exclusion*. Ithaca, NY: Cornell University Press.

Fenton, N. (2009). My media studies: getting political in a global, digital age. *Television & New Media*, 10(1), 55–7. https://doi.org/10.1177/1527476408325100

Fernandes, F. (2008). *A integração do negro na sociedade de classes*, 5th edn. Rio de Janeiro: Globo. E-book.

Fisher, M. (2009). *Capitalist realism: Is there no alternative?* Ropley: ZerO Books.

Foucault, M. (1972). *The archaeology of knowledge*. London: Tavistock Publications.

Foucault, M. (1979a). *Discipline and punish: The birth of the prison*. Harmondsworth: Penguin Books.

Foucault, M. (1979b). *Microfísica do poder*. Rio de Janeiro: Graal.

Foucault, M. (1988). *História da sexualidade I*. São Paulo: Editora Graal.

Fraser, N. (1995). From redistribution to recognition? Dilemmas of justice in a 'post-socialist' age. *New Left Review*, 212, July/August, 68–93.

References

Fraser, N. (2000). Rethinking recognition. *New Left Review*, 3, May/June, 107–20.

Freire, P. (2005). *Pedagogia do oprimido*. Rio de Janeiro: Paz e Terra.

Freire Filho, J. (2012). Big Brother Brasil e o valor da autenticidade. In: França, V., & Corrêa, L. (eds.) *Mídia, instituições e valores* (pp. 53–66). Belo Horizonte: Autêntica.

Frier, S. (2020). *No filter: The inside story of Instagram*. New York: Simon & Schuster.

Gamson, J. (1994). *Claims to fame: Celebrity in contemporary America*. Berkeley: University of California Press.

Gerlitz, C., & Helmond, A. (2013). The like economy: Social buttons and the data-intensive Web. *New Media & Society*, 15(8), 1348–65. https://doi.org/10.1177/1461444812472322

Gershon, I. (2011). Un-friend my heart: Facebook, promiscuity, and heartbreak in a neoliberal age. *Anthropological Quarterly*, 84(4), 865–94. https://doi.org/10.1353/anq.2011.0048

Gibson, J. J. (1979). *The ecological approach to visual perception*. Boston: Houghton Mifflin.

Gillespie, T. (2010). The politics of 'platforms'. *New Media & Society*, 12(3), 347–64. https://doi.org/10.1177/1461444809342738

Glatt, Z. (2022). Media and uncertainty. 'We're all told not to put our eggs in one basket': uncertainty, precarity and cross-platform labor in the online video influencer industry. *International Journal of Communication*, 16, 19. https://ijoc.org/index.php/ijoc/article/view/15761

Goffman, E. (1983). *A representação do eu na vida cotidiana*. Petrópolis: Vozes.

Greenhow, C., & Lewin, C. (2016). Social media and education: reconceptualizing the boundaries of formal

References

and informal learning. *Learning, Media and Technology*, 41(1), 6–30.

Grosser, B. (2014). What do metrics want? How quantification prescribes social interaction on Facebook. *Computational Culture*, 4. Retrieved from http://computationalculture.net/what-do-metrics-want/ (accessed 1 June 2023)

Hacking, I. (1990). *The taming of chance: Ideas in context*. Cambridge: Cambridge University Press.

Hall, S. (2021). *Selected writings on race and difference*. Edited by P. Gilroy & R. Gilmore. Durham, NC and London: Duke University Press.

Hall, S., & Du Gay, P. (1996). *Questions of cultural identity*. London: Sage.

Hampton, K., Rainie, L., Lu, W., Shin, I., & Purcell, K. (2015). Psychological stress and social media use. Retrieved from https://www.pewresearch.org/internet/2015/01/15/psychological-stress-and-social-media-use-2/ (accessed 1 June 2023)

Hearn, A. (2017). Verified: self-presentation, identity management, and selfhood in the age of big data. *Popular Communication*, 15(2), 62–77. https://doi.org/10.1080/15405702.2016.1269909

Hegde, R. S. (ed.) (2011). *Circuits of visibility: Gender and transnational media cultures*. New York: NYU Press.

Hegel, G. W. F. (1977). *The phenomenology of spirit*. Translated by A. V. Miller. Oxford: Oxford University Press.

Hegel, G. W. F. (1983). *Hegel and the human spirit: A translation of the Jena Lectures on the Philosophy of Spirit (1805–6) with commentary*. Translated by L. Rauch. Detroit, MI: Wayne State University Press.

Heinich, N. (2012). *De la visibilité: excellence et singularité en régime médiatique*. Paris: Gallimard.

Heller, D. (ed.) (2006). *The great American makeover:*

References

Television, history, nation. New York: Palgrave Macmillan.

Hepp, A. (2009). Differentiation: mediatization and cultural change. In: Lunby, K. (ed.) *Mediatization: Concept, changes, consequences* (pp. 139–57). New York: Peter Lang.

Herdzina, J., & Lauricella, A. R. (2020). *Media literacy in early childhood report.* Chicago: Technology in Early Childhood (TEC) Center, Erikson Institute.

Hjarvard, S. (2008). The mediatization of society: a theory of the media as agents of social and cultural change. *Nordicom Review*, 29(2), 105–34.

Hjarvard, S. (2014). Mediatization and cultural and social change: an institutional perspective. In: Lunby, K. (ed.) *Mediatization of communication* (pp. 199–226). Berlin: De Gruyter Mouton.

Hobbes, T. (1991). *Leviathan.* Cambridge: Cambridge University Press.

Holiday, S., Norman, M. S., & Densley, R. L. (2020). Sharenting and the extended self: self-representation in parents' Instagram presentations of their children. *Popular Communication*, 20(1), 1–15. https://doi.org/10.1080/15405702.2020.1744610

Honneth, A. (1995). *The struggle for recognition: The moral grammar of social conflicts.* Cambridge, MA: MIT Press.

Honneth, A. (2008). *Reification: A new look at an old idea.* Oxford: Oxford University Press.

Honneth, A. (2014). *Freedom's right: The social foundations of democratic life.* New York: Columbia University Press.

Honneth, A., & Margalit, A. (2001). Recognition. *Proceedings of the Aristotelian Society*, 75 (Suppl.), 111–39.

Humphreys, L. (2018). *The qualified self: Social media*

References

and the accounting of everyday life. Cambridge, MA: MIT Press.

Ifergan, P. (2014). *Hegel's discovery of the philosophy of spirit: Autonomy, alienation and the ethical life: The Jena Lectures 1802–1806.* New York: Palgrave Macmillan.

Ikäheimo, H. (2015). Conceptualizing causes for lack of recognition: capacities, costs and understanding. *Studies in Social and Political Thought*, 250. https://doi.org/10.20919/sspt.25.2015.45

Ikäheimo, H., & Laitinen, A. (2007). Analyzing recognition: identification, acknowledgement, and recognitive attitudes towards persons. In: Van den Brink, B., & Owen, D. (eds.) *Recognition and power: Axel Honneth and the tradition of critical social theory* (pp. 33–56). Cambridge: Cambridge University Press.

Illouz, E. (2011). *O amor nos tempos de capitalismo.* Rio de Janeiro: Jorge Zahar Editor.

Innis, H. A. (1951). *The bias of communication.* Toronto: University of Toronto Press.

Jenkins, H. (2006). *Convergence culture: Where old media meets new media.* New York: NYU Press.

Jenkins, H., Shresthova, S., Gamber-Thompson, L., Kligler-Vilenchik, N., & Zimmerman, A. (2016). *By any media necessary: The new youth activism.* New York: NYU Press.

Jermyn D. (2021). Barefaced: Ageing women stars, 'no make-up' photography and authentic selfhood in the 2017 Pirelli calendar. *European Journal of Cultural Studies*, 24(5), 1125–42. https://doi.org/10.1177/1367549420919891

Johnson, S. A. (2014). 'Maternal devices', social media and the self-management of pregnancy, mothering and child health. *Societies*, 4(2), 330–50. https://doi.org/10.3390/soc4020330

References

Jones, S. (1998). *Virtual culture: Identity and communication in cyberspace.* Thousand Oaks, CA: Sage.

Jorge, A., Marôpo, L., Coelho, A. M., & Novello, L. (2022). Mummy influencers and professional sharenting. *European Journal of Cultural Studies,* 25(1), 166–82. https://doi.org/10.1177/13675494211004593

Jorge, A., Marôpo, L., & Nunes, T. (2018). 'I am not being sponsored to say this': a teen YouTuber and her audience negotiate branded content. *Observatorio (OBS*).* https://doi.org/10.15847/obsOBS0001382

Kallen, E. (2004). *Social inequality and social injustice: A human rights perspective.* New York: Palgrave Macmillan.

Karppi, T. (2018). *Disconnect: Facebook affective bonds.* Minneapolis: University of Minnesota Press.

Kellner, D. (1995). *Media culture: Cultural studies, identity and politics between the modern and the postmodern.* London: Routledge.

Khamis, S., Ang, L., & Welling, R. (2017). Self-branding, 'microcelebrity' and the rise of social media influencers. *Celebrity Studies,* 8(2), 191–208. https://doi.org/10.1080/19392397.2016.1218292

King, B. (1987). The star and the commodity: notes towards a performance theory of stardom. *Cultural Studies,* 1(2), 145–61. https://doi.org/10.1080/09502388700490111

King, B. (2008). Stardom, celebrity and the para-confession. *Social Semiotics,* 18(2), 115–32. https://doi.org/10.1080/10350330802002135

Kiziltunali, G. (2016). Simulated identities: social media and the reconciliation of the real and ideal. *Media Psychology Review,* 10(1). Retrieved from https://mprcenter.org/review/simulated-identities-social-media-and-the-reconciliation-of-the-real-and-ideal/ (accessed 3 June 2023)

Kramer, A., Guillory, J., & Hancock, J. (2014). Experimental

References

evidence of massive-scale emotional contagion through social networks. *Proceedings of the National Academy of Sciences*, 111(24), 8788–90. https://doi.org/10.1073/pnas.1320040111

Krotz, F. (2007). The meta-process of 'mediatization' as a conceptual frame. *Global Media and Communication*, 3(3), 256–60. https://doi.org/10.1177/17427665070030030103

Kuehn, K., & Corrigan, T. (2013). Hope labor: the role of employment prospects in online social production. *The Political Economy of Communication*, 1(1), 9–25.

Kuntsman, A. (2017). Introduction: whose selfie citizenship? In: Kuntsman A. (ed.) *Selfie citizenship* (pp. 13–18). Cham: Palgrave Macmillan.

Kuntsman, A., & Miyake, E. (2019). The paradox and continuum of digital disengagement: denaturalising digital sociality and technological connectivity. *Media, Culture & Society*, 41(6), 901–13. https://doi.org/10.1177/0163443719853732

Lahire, B. (2004). *Retratos sociológicos: disposições e variações individuais*. Porto Alegre: Artmed.

Lash, C. (1991). *The culture of narcissism: American life in an age of diminishing expectations*. New York: Norton.

Lenoir, R. (1974). *Les exclus, un Français sur dix*. Paris: Editions du Seuil.

Lévy, P. (1999a). *Cibercultura*. São Paulo: Editora 34.

Lévy, P. (1999b). *Collective intelligence: Mankind's emerging world in cyberspace*. New York: Perseus Books.

Lim, E. (2021). Personal identity economics: Facebook and the distortion of identity politics. *Social Media + Society*, 7(2). https://doi.org/10.1177/20563051211017492

Livingstone, S. (2003). The changing nature and uses of media literacy. *Media@LSE Electronic Working Papers*, No. 4. Retrieved from http://eprints.lse.ac.uk/13476

References

/1/The_changing_nature_and_uses_of_media_literacy.pdf (accessed 1 June 2023)

Livingstone, S. (2007). The challenge of engaging youth online: contrasting producers' and teenagers' interpretations of websites. *European Journal of Communication*, 22(2), 165–84. https://doi.org/10.1177/0267323107076768

Livingstone, S. (2008). Taking risky opportunities in youthful content creation: teenagers' use of social networking sites for intimacy, privacy and self-expression. *New Media & Society*, 10(3), 393–411.

Livingstone, S. (2011). Internet literacy: a negociação dos jovens com as novas oportunidades on-line. *Revista Matrizes*, 4(2), 11–42. https://doi.org/10.11606/issn.1982-8160.v4i2p11-42

Livingstone, S. (2019). Audiences in an age of datafication: critical questions for media research. *Television & New Media*, 20(2), 170–83. https://doi.org/10.1177/1527476418811118

Lorenzana, J. (2016). Mediated recognition: The role of Facebook in identity and social formations of Filipino transnationals in Indian cities. *New Media & Society*, 18(10), 2189–206. https://doi.org/10.1177/1461444816655613

Lowenthal, L. (2006). The triumph of mass idols. In: Marshall, P. D. (ed.) *The celebrity culture reader* (pp. 124–52). New York: Routledge.

Luke, C. (1989). *Pedagogy, printing and Protestantism: The discourse of childhood*. Albany, NY: State University of New York Press.

Machiavelli, N. (1988). *The prince*. Cambridge: Cambridge University Press.

Magalhães, J. C. (2019). *Voice through silence: Algorithmic visibility, ordinary civic voices and bottom-up authoritarianism in the Brazilian crisis*. PhD thesis, London School of Economics and Political Science.

References

Maia, R. (2014). *Recognition and the media*. New York: Palgrave Macmillan.

Malik, S. (2014). Diversity, broadcasting and the politics of representation. In: Horsti, K., Hultén, G., & Titley, G. (eds.) *National conversations: Public service media and cultural diversity in Europe* (pp. 21–41). Bristol: Intellect.

Marshall, P. D. (1997). *Celebrity and power: Fame in contemporary culture*. Minneapolis: University of Minnesota Press.

Marshall, T. H. (1950). *Citizenship and social class: And other essays*. Cambridge: Cambridge University Press.

Martins, R., & Bastos, A. (2017). O reconhecimento como ideologia e os papeis dos media na representação da mulher. *Vozes e Diálogo*, 16(2).

Marwick, A. E. (2013). *Status update: Celebrity, publicity, and branding in the social media age*. New Haven, CT: Yale University Press.

Mattos, P. (2006). *A sociologia política do reconhecimento: as contribuições de Charles Taylor, Axel Honneth e Nancy Fraser*. São Paulo: Annablume.

Mayer-Schönberger, V., & Cukier, K. (2013). *Big data: A revolution that will transform how we live, work, and think*. London: John Murray.

McBride, C. (2013). *Recognition*. Cambridge: Polity.

McLuhan, M. (1967). *Understanding media: The extension of man*. London: Sphere Books.

Meikle, G. (2016). *Social media: Communication, sharing and visibility*. New York: Routledge.

Mendonça, R. F. (2011). Recognition and social esteem: a case study of the struggles of people affected by leprosy. *Political Studies*, 59(4), 940–58.

Meyrowitz, J. (1985). *No sense of place*. Oxford: Oxford University Press.

Miller, T. (2008). *Makeover nation*. Columbus: The Ohio State University Press.

References

Mitra, A. (2001). Marginal voices in cyberspace. *New Media & Society*, 3(1), 29–48. https://doi.org/10.1177/1461444801003001003

Muscat, T. (2019). Misrecognising the value of voice: anticipating inclusion beyond mainstream mediations of race and migration. *Media, Culture & Society*, 41(8), 1160–75. https://doi.org/10.1177/0163443719842077

Nærland, T. (2019). Altogether now? Symbolic recognition, musical media events and the forging of civic bonds among minority youth in Norway. *European Journal of Cultural Studies*, 22(1), 78–94. https://doi.org/10.1177/1367549417719013

Negroponte, N. (1995). *Being digital*. London: Hodder and Stoughton.

Nemer, D., & Freeman, G. (2015). Empowering the marginalized: rethinking selfies in the slums of Brazil. *International Journal of Communication*, 9(1), 1832–47.

Nikunen, K. (2019). Once a refugee: selfie activism, visualized citizenship and the space of appearance. *Popular Communication*, 17(2), 154–70. https://doi.org/10.1080/15405702.2018.1527336

Noble, G. (2009). 'Countless acts of recognition': young men, ethnicity and the messiness of identities in everyday life. *Social & Cultural Geography*, 10(8), 875–91. https://doi.org/10.1080/14649360903305767

Nunes, W. (2018). Curso do Whindersson. Retrieved from https://web.archive.org/web/20200813054231/http://cursodowhindersson.com.br/blog/inscricao/ (accessed 25 May 2023)

Ormerod, K. (2020). *Why social media is ruining your life*. New York: Octopus Books.

Ouellette, L., & Hay, J. (2008). *Better living through reality TV: Television and post-welfare citizenship*. Oxford: Blackwell.

Paasonen, S. (2021). *Dependent, distracted, bored:*

References

Affective formations in networked media. Cambridge, MA: MIT Press.

Pakulski, J. (1997). Cultural citizenship. *Citizenship Studies*, 1(1), 73–86. http://dx.doi.org/10.1080/1362102 9708420648

Peters, J. D. (1999). *Speaking into the air: A history of the idea of communication*. Chicago: The University of Chicago Press.

Peters, J. D. (2015). *The marvelous clouds: Towards a philosophy of elemental media*. Chicago: The University of Chicago Press.

Philips, D. (2005). Transformation scenes: the television interior makeover. *International Journal of Cultural Studies*, 8(2), 213–29. https://doi.org/10.1177/1367877905052418

Plessner, H. (1970). *Philosophische Anthropologie*. Frankfurt am Main: Fischer.

Polivanov, B., & Carrera, F. (2019). Rupturas performáticas em sites de redes sociais: um olhar sobre fissuras no processo de apresentação de si a partir de e para além de Goffman. *Intexto*, 44, 74–98. http://dx.doi.org/10.19132/1807-8583201944.74-98

Puschmann, C., & Bozdag, E. (2014). Staking out the unclear ethical terrain of online social experiments. *Internet Policy Review*, 3(4). https://doi.org/10.14763/2014.4.338

Qiu, L., Lin, H., Leung, A. K., & Tov, W. (2012). Putting their best foot forward: emotional disclosure on Facebook. *Cyberpsychology, Behavior and Social Networking*, 15(10), 569–72. https://doi.org/10.1089/cyber.2012.0200

Raisborough, J. (2011). *Lifestyle media and the formation of the self*. New York: Palgrave Macmillan.

Rancière, J. (2009). *A partilha do sensível: estética e política*. São Paulo: Editora 34.

References

Reade, J. (2021). Keeping it raw on the 'gram': authenticity, relatability and digital intimacy in fitness cultures on Instagram. *New Media & Society*, 23(3), 535–53. https://doi.org/10.1177/1461444819891699

Rheingold, H. (1994). *The virtual community*. London: Martin Secker & Warburg.

Rieder, B., Matamoros-Fernández, A., & Coromina, Ò. (2018). From ranking algorithms to 'ranking cultures': investigating the modulation of visibility in YouTube search results. *Convergence*, 24(1), 50–68. https://doi.org/10.1177/1354856517736982

Ringmar, E. (2002). The recognition game: Soviet Russia against the West. *Cooperation and Conflict*, 37(2), 115–36.

Rojek, C. (2001). *Celebrity*. London: Reaktion Books.

Said, E. (2003). *Orientalism*. London: Penguin Books.

Sanches, T. (2022). *Lutas por reconhecimento e moradia espacial em Londres e Rio de Janeiro*. Rio de Janeiro: Appris Editora.

Schäfer, M. T., & Van Es, K. (2017). *The datafied society: Studying culture through data*. Amsterdam: Amsterdam University Press.

Schroeder, R. (2014). Big Data and the brave new world of social media research. *Big Data & Society*, 1(2). https://doi.org/10.1177/2053951714563194

Schulz, C. (2023). A new algorithmic imaginary. *Media, Culture & Society*, 45(3), 646–55. https://doi.org/10.1177/01634437221136014

Scolari, C. (2018). *Literacia transmedia na nova ecologia mediática: Livro Branco*. Barcelona: European Union Funding for Research & Innovation.

Scolere, L., Pruchniewska, U., & Duffy, B. E. (2018). Constructing the platform-specific self-brand: the labor of social media promotion. *Social Media + Society*, 4(3). https://doi.org/10.1177/2056305118784768

References

Senft, T. (2013). Microcelebrity and the branded self. In: Hartley, J., Burgess, J., & Bruns, A. (eds.) *A companion to new media dynamics* (pp. 346–54). Malden, MA: Wiley.

Sennett, R. (2001). *O declínio do homem publico: as tiranias da intimidade*. São Paulo: Companhia das Letras.

Serelle, M., & Sena, E. (2019). Crítica e reconhecimento: lutas identitárias na cultura midiática. *MATRIZes*, 13(1), 149–67. https://doi.org/10.11606/issn.1982-8160.v13i1p149-167

Simmel, G. (1973). A metrópole e a vida mental. In: Velho, G. (ed.) *O fenômeno urbano* (pp. 11–25). Rio de Janeiro: Zafar Editores.

Skeggs, B. (2014). Values beyond value? Is anything beyond the logic of capital? *The British Journal of Sociology*, 65(1), 1–20. https://doi.org/10.1111/1468-4446.12072

Skeggs, B. (2015). A economia moral da apresentação pessoal: relações de classe e auto-performances nos reality shows. *Revista Parágrafo*, 1(3).

Souza, J. (2003). *A construção social da subcidadania: para uma sociologia política da modernidade periférica*. Belo Horizonte: Editora UFMG.

Souza, J. (2011). The singularity of peripheral social inequality. In: Levy, J., & Young, M. (eds.) *Colonialism and its legacies* (pp. 121–45). Plymouth: Lexington Books.

Souza, J. (2012). *Os batalhadores brasileiros: nova classe media ou nova classe trabalhadora?* Belo Horizonte: Editora UFMG.

Souza, J. (2018). *A ralé brasileira: quem é e como vive*. São Paulo: Editora Contracorrente.

Spivak, G. C. (1988). Can the subaltern speak? In: Nelson, C., & Grossberg, L. (eds.) *Marxism and the*

References

interpretation of culture (pp. 271–313). Champaign: University of Illinois Press.

Standlee, A. (2019). Friendship and online filtering: the use of social media to construct offline social networks. *New Media & Society*, 21(3), 770–85. https://doi.org/10.1177/1461444818806844

Stevenson, N. (2001). Culture and citizenship: an introduction. In: Stevenson, N. (ed.) *Culture and citizenship* (pp. 1–10). London: Sage.

Taylor, C. (1991). *The ethics of authenticity*. Cambridge, MA: Harvard University Press.

Taylor, C. (1994). *Multiculturalism: Examining the politics of recognition*. Princeton, NJ: Princeton University Press.

Taylor, C. (2001). *Sources of the self: The making of modern identity*. Cambridge, MA: Harvard University Press.

Taylor, C. (2004). *Modern social imaginaries*. Durham, NC and London: Duke University Press.

Thatcher, J., O'Sullivan, D., & Mahmoudi, D. (2016). Data colonialism through accumulation by dispossession: new metaphors for daily data. *Environment and Planning D: Society and Space*, 34(6), 990–1006. https://doi.org/10.1177/0263775816633195

Thompson, E. P. (1963). *The making of the English working class*. London: Vintage Books.

Thumim, N (2012). *Self-representation and digital culture*. New York: Palgrave Macmillan.

Tomaz, R. (2019). *O que você vai ser antes de crescer? Youtubers, infância e celebridade*. Salvador: EDUFBA.

Trilling, L. (1972). *Sincerity and authenticity*. Cambridge, MA: Harvard University Press.

Turkle, S. (1996). *Life on the screen*. London: Weidenfeld & Nicolson.

Turner, G. (2004). *Understanding celebrity*. London: Sage.

References

Turner, G. (2010). *Ordinary people and the media: The demotic turn*. London: Sage.

Turner, V. (1974). *Dramas, fields and metaphors*. Ithaca, NY: Cornell University Press.

UNESCO. (1983). The Grünwald Declaration on media education. *Educational Media International*, 20(3), 26. https://doi.org/10.1080/09523988308549128

Van Dijck, J., Poell, T., & De Waal, M. (2018). *The platform society: Public values in a connective world*. New York: Oxford University Press.

Van Krieken, R. (2012). *Celebrity society*. London: Routledge.

Vriens, E., & Van Ingen, E. (2018). Does the rise of the Internet bring erosion of strong ties? Analyses of social media use and changes in core discussion networks. *New Media & Society*, 20(7), 2432–49. https://doi.org/10.1177/1461444817724169

Warwick-Booth, L. (2013). *Social inequality*. London: Sage.

Waterloo, S. F., Baumgartner, S. E., Peter, J., & Valkenburg, P. M. (2018). Norms of online expressions of emotion: comparing Facebook, Twitter, Instagram, and WhatsApp. *New Media & Society*, 20(5), 1813–31. https://doi.org/10.1177/1461444817707349

Weber, B. (2009). *Makeover TV: Selfhood, citizenship, and celebrity*. Durham, NC and London: Duke University Press.

Weber, M. (1958). Religious rejections of the world and their directions. In: Gerth, H. H., & Wright Mills, C. (eds.) *From Max Weber: Essays in sociology* (pp. 323–59). New York: Oxford University Press.

Weinstein, E. (2018). The social media see-saw: positive and negative influences on adolescents' affective well-being. *New Media & Society*, 20(10), 3597–623. https://doi.org/10.1177/1461444818755634

References

Wouters, C. (2007). *Informalization: Manners and emotions since 1890*. Los Angeles: Sage.

Zuboff, S. (2019). *The age of surveillance capitalism: The fight for a human future at the new frontier of power*. New York: Public Affairs.

Index

Abidin, Crystal, 136–7, 138
acknowledgement, 16–17
activism, 28, 99, 108
adaptability, 10, 107, 132, 134
administrative disposition, 114
affection, 8, 9, 12, 21, 28, 83, 97–8
affinity scores, 79–80, 124
Agamben, Giorgio, 101–2
agency, 49, 58, 65, 103, 134
Ajana, Btihaj, 77–8
algorithmic imaginaries, 52, 134, 137
algorithms, 7, 45, 52, 58–61, 72, 76, 79–80, 88–9, 102–7, 123–9, 134, 137, 141–5, 149
alienation, 18, 85
Andersen, Jack, 69–70

Araújo, Willian, 83, 103–4, 105
Aristotle, 18
art, 18, 91, 112
artificial intelligence, 79
authenticity, 31, 33, 57, 86, 90–3, 104–5, 125, 126, 129, 139
authoritarianism, 144, 147
authority, 5, 6, 55, 120
autonomy, 18, 25, 35–6, 142, 144–5, 147

backstage, 95–6
Bakhtin, Mikhail, 55
Balleys, Claire, 56–8, 59, 84, 130, 131
Barassi, Veronica, 141, 142
Baym, Nancy K., 13
behaviour manuals, 9, 83, 86–90, 94, 104, 149
Bell, Catherine, 66, 69

Index

Bentham, Jeremy, 72–3
Berger, Peter, 22, 61
Biressi, Anita, 110–11, 138, 142
Bishop, Sophie, 59
#BlackLivesMatter movement, 38
Boltanski, Luc, 115–16, 117, 132, 146
Bourdieu, Pierre, 33, 36–8, 112, 114, 123, 139–40
bourgeois society, 22, 34, 39, 91–2
branding *see* self-branding
Bucher, Taina, 62, 72–3, 78–9, 80

cancel culture, 105
capitalism, 26, 36, 43, 55, 72, 74, 98, 106, 113, 115–16, 138, 149
celebrities, 12–14, 28–30, 56, 67–8, 90, 92–3, 105, 123, 134
Chambers, Deborah, 142–3
Chiapello, Eve, 115–16, 117, 132, 146
childhood, 21, 131
Chouliaraki, Lilie, 28
citizenship, 2, 5, 10, 23, 25, 33–4, 37–43, 49, 94, 109–13, 118, 120, 128, 131–4, 140–9
civic value, 5, 10, 129, 141, 143–4, 146, 147
civil rights, 11, 142, 150
civilization, 86–7, 91–2, 104

collectivity, 11, 55, 109
colonialism, 34, 35, 43
comments, 3, 13, 45, 57, 74, 79, 104, 109, 124, 127, 130, 141
commodification, 75, 99, 135, 149
competition, 19, 40, 41, 117, 132
conditional recognition, 28–9
conflict, 6, 11, 18, 20, 36, 52, 135
consumption, 15, 59, 140
Cornell University, 70–1
Cottle, Simon, 49–50, 133
Couldry, Nick, 1, 48, 49, 53–4, 61, 62, 65–9, 98, 126
court society, 86, 91–3, 95
COVID-19 pandemic, 14–15, 64
Creator Academy, 103
Cukier, Kenneth, 4
cultural citizenship, 2, 25, 141, 143
cultural rights, 11, 150
curation, 7, 61–2, 71, 76, 149

data collection, 46, 59, 61, 69, 74, 142
data colonialism, 43
Data Overview Report, 148
datafication, 4–5, 9, 15, 36, 43, 45–6, 61–9, 76, 83, 117, 143–6, 149

Index

datafied habitus, 4–5, 10–11, 15, 100, 105, 107, 121–2, 128–30, 137–41, 146–7, 149
datafied logics, 6, 86, 126, 132, 146
dating sites, 98–9
De Civilitate Morum Puerilium (Erasmus), 83, 86–8, 93, 104
De Vito, Michael A., 79
deep mediatization, 69–70
deliberation, 23, 26, 48, 50, 52, 53, 84, 141
democracy, 7, 23, 47, 49, 120, 144
democratization, 72, 85, 92–3, 126–7, 150
Desmurget, Michel, 2
difference, 31–2, 36–7, 41–2, 50, 75
digital assistants, 15
'digital detox', 81, 127
dignity, 22, 32, 33, 34–6, 38, 39, 42, 75, 140, 147
disciplinary power, 84–6, 101
dispositions, 3, 9–10, 15, 36, 40, 105, 107–35, 137, 140–1, 143, 146, 149
dispositives, 78, 101–2, 105
disrespect, 6, 52, 144, 145
Duarte, Luiz Fernando, 40
Duffy, Brooke Erin, 54, 110, 138
Durkheim, Émile, 68

economic disposition, 114
economic value, 9, 45–6, 54, 74
EdgeRank, 79
edges, 78–9
education, 23, 31–2, 115, 119, 121–2
Edwards, Lee, 1, 50
Elias, Norbert, 22, 65, 83, 86–7, 91–3, 94, 97, 104
emotion, 13, 21, 28, 70–1, 83, 88, 91–5, 97–8, 134–8, 145
'emotional contagion' project, 70–1
engagement, 5, 71, 72, 78–82, 145, 148, 149
Enlightenment, 18, 34
entrepreneurship, 5, 10, 85–6, 107, 132, 134, 138, 139, 141, 142
equality, 3, 22–5, 32, 37–8, 42, 75, 106, 126–8, 131, 134, 144, 149
Erasmus, 83, 86–8, 93, 104, 149
esteem, 1, 8, 9, 24–5, 27, 29, 53, 57, 72, 131, 150; *see also* self-esteem; social esteem
ethnography, 17, 53
evaluation, 7, 37, 80, 109–10
exclusion, 41, 48, 115–17, 142–3, 146–7
expertise, 85, 88
exploitation, 35, 115, 117

179

Index

expressive gestures of recognition, 72, 74–5, 80, 130–1, 134
expressive self, 33, 36, 42

Facebook, 44, 53, 57–62, 70–6, 78–80, 84, 99–100, 102, 109, 125, 126, 132, 136, 144–5, 147
facial recognition, 17
Faimau, Gabriel, 1
family, 20–1, 116
fans, 12–13, 28–9, 67–8, 110
far-right politics, 128–9
feedback, 7–8, 78
feminism, 36, 99
Fenton, Natalie, 141
figurations, 65–6, 69, 84
film, 50–1, 96
flexibility, 10, 41, 107, 132, 134, 138
followers, 3, 7, 10, 12–13, 29, 59, 74, 90, 93, 109, 129
Foucault, Michel, 39, 72–3, 101, 138
framing, 50, 51, 54, 66–7, 69, 84, 85
Frankfurt School, 51
Fraser, Nancy, 32–3
freedom, 3, 7, 11, 18, 20, 22, 26, 49, 90, 97, 118, 131, 134, 135, 150
Freeman, Guo, 107
Freud, Sigmund, 21

friendships, 7, 20–1, 65–6, 129, 136, 143
Frier, Sarah, 127, 137
frontstage, 95–6

gender, 17, 50–1, 59, 97, 99, 139, 142, 147
Gerlitz, Carolin, 78
Gillespie, Tarleton, 58–9
Glatt, Zoë, 110, 138
Global North, 34, 36, 38, 146
Global South, 33–7, 41, 140, 146
Goethe, Johann Wolfgang von, 91
Goffman, Erving, 95–6
Greenhow, Christine, 120
Grosser, Benjamin, 80

habitus, 4–5, 8, 10–11, 15, 37–43, 92, 94–5, 101, 105, 107, 112, 117–22, 128–30, 134, 137–47, 149; *see also* datafied habitus; primary habitus
Hacking, Ian, 77, 78
Hall, Stuart, 55
hashtags, 12, 67, 103
Hay, James, 142
Hearn, Alison, 84, 127
Hegel, G. W. F., 6, 18, 19–20, 26, 30, 46–7
Heinich, Natalie, 123–4
Helmond, Anne, 78
Hepp, Andreas, 3, 61, 62, 64–6, 69

180

Index

hierarchies, 2, 11, 22, 37, 85, 125–30, 132, 134–5
Hjarvard, Stig, 63–4
Hobbes, Thomas, 19
Honneth, Axel, 1, 6, 8, 16, 19–27, 30, 33, 45, 48–51, 72–5, 99, 101, 106, 118, 128, 130–1, 150
honour, 22, 24, 42
horizontal recognition, 27
humanitarianism, 28
HypeAuditor, 81

ideal self, 99, 101
identification, 16–17, 60
identity formation, 4, 5–6, 15, 21, 40, 42, 43, 50, 52–3, 56–8, 98, 130
identity politics, 30–3, 46
Ifergan, Pini, 19
Ikäheimo, Heikki, 16–17, 27
Illouz, Eva, 97–9, 123
inclusion, 23, 41, 51–2, 115, 118, 142, 146–7, 148
indigenous peoples, 25, 31, 49, 133
individuality, 24, 25, 31–2, 42, 141
individualization, 5, 25, 63, 129, 135, 143
inequality, 32, 36, 37, 125, 139, 140, 142, 147
influencers, 5, 29–30, 83, 88–90, 92, 105, 107, 123, 136–7

informalization, 93–5, 105, 129
Innis, Harold, 63
Instagram, 12, 44, 74–6, 81, 100, 102, 108, 109, 121, 124–5, 127, 136, 137
institutions of recognition, 1–2, 26
instrumentalization, 2, 9, 29
intimacy, 56, 58, 97, 129, 130
invisibility, 49, 62, 73, 116, 145
Islamophobia, 48

Jenkins, Henry, 54–5, 120
Jolie, Angelina, 28

Kant, Emmanuel, 91
Karppi, Tero, 106
Kelly, Kevin, 76–7
Kramer, Adam D. I., 70–1
Kreckel, Reinhard, 39–40, 42
Krotz, Friedrich, 63
Kuntsman, Adi, 109, 143

labour, 13, 35, 36, 40, 41, 115, 117, 138, 146
Lahire, Bernard, 113, 114
Latinen, Arto, 16–17
legal relations, 20, 22–4, 27
Lenoir, René, 116
Lévy, Pierre, 55
Lewin, Cathy, 120

Index

LGBTQ people, 25, 31, 32–3, 36, 50–1, 147
'likes', 3, 7, 45, 57, 72, 74, 78, 79, 80–1, 109, 130, 141, 145
liveness, 67–8
Livingstone, Sonia, 64, 119–20
Locke, John, 34
Lorenzana, Jozon A., 1, 45, 53, 57, 59, 84, 131
love, 20–1, 26, 27, 85, 142
Lowenthal, Leo, 110, 111
Luckmann, Thomas, 61

Machiavelli, Niccolo, 18–19
machine learning, 6–7
Magalhães, João Carlos Vieira, 104, 105, 144–7
Maia, Rousiley, 1, 45, 51–2, 53, 59, 84, 133
makeover shows, 85, 142
Malik, Sarita, 48–9, 133
Margalit, Avishai, 72–3, 130–1
marginalized groups, 2, 11, 50–2, 55, 73–5, 97, 115, 133, 134, 142, 146, 150; *see also* minority groups
market economy, 1, 26, 29, 138, 142
Marshall, P. D., 94
Marshall, T. H., 23, 25
Marwick, Alice E., 138–9, 141
Marx, Karl, 26

Marxism, 115
mass media, 6, 44, 50–4, 61, 66–8, 75, 86, 96–7, 119–20, 133, 141–2; *see also* newspapers; radio; television
Mayer-Schönberger, Viktor, 4
McBride, Cillian, 24
McLuhan, Marshall, 63
Mead, George, 22
media literacy, 100, 118–22
media logics, 63, 64
mediated centre, 67–8
mediatization, 62, 63–70
Mejias, Ulises Ali, 53–4, 68–9
mental health, 81
meritocracy, 40, 138, 139, 142
meta-capital, 59–60, 67, 123
#MeToo movement, 2, 38
metrics, 4, 54, 76–82, 84, 134, 141; *see also* quantification
Meyrowitz, Joshua, 63
migration, 36
minority groups, 11, 25, 31–2, 36, 48–52, 73–4, 97, 115, 133, 150; *see also* marginalized groups
Mitra, Ananda, 55
modernity, 18, 22, 90, 97
monetization, 15, 59, 78, 137
morality, 15, 17, 22, 28, 33–9, 42, 75, 110, 130, 134, 149

Index

multiculturalism, 30–2, 33, 36, 41–2, 49
Muscat, Tanya, 48
Musk, Elon, 125
mutual recognition, 19–20, 36

Nærland, Torgeir Uberg, 1
national identity, 91
negative rights, 22
Nemer, David, 108
neoliberalism, 3, 10, 15, 85–6, 107, 136–9, 142
networks, 116–17
news feeds, 7, 9, 44–6, 61–2, 69–76, 79–82, 84, 90, 103, 124–5, 129, 144–5, 147, 149
newspapers, 2, 47–8, 50, 51, 53, 67, 119, 133
Nikunen, Kaarina, 1, 108
Noble, Greg, 17
Nunes, Whindersson, 83, 88–90, 92, 102–3, 104–5
Nunn, Heather, 142

objectification, 9, 66, 78, 129, 132
oral culture, 119, 121
Ormerod, Katherine, 2
other, the, 19–20, 27–8, 38, 47, 48–50, 55
Ouellette, Laurie, 142

Paasonen, Susanna, 106
Pakulski, Jan, 25, 141
panopticon, 72–3

performance, 12–13, 28–9, 39–40, 42, 93, 95–6, 102
permanent connection, 10, 65, 107, 122–30, 134
personal data, 7, 43, 142
Peters, John, 46–7, 63
Philips, Deborah, 85
Plessner, Helmuth, 74
political listening, 48
political mobilization, 54–5
political participation, 23
political rights, 11, 150
Pooley, Jefferson, 54, 110, 138
Popuzuda, Valesca, 13
positive rights, 22–3
postcolonial studies, 97
power, 5–6, 9, 15, 19, 51–5, 59–60, 64–7, 71, 73, 83–6, 94, 98, 100–2, 105, 123, 143, 149
precarity, 36, 40–1, 43, 110, 117, 118, 135, 146
primary habitus, 38–41, 43, 112, 117, 118, 137–8, 140, 146
private sphere, 14, 98
promotion campaigns, 12–13
psychoanalysis, 98
public relations, 50
public service broadcasting, 48–9
public sphere, 14, 26, 64, 75, 98
punctual self, 33, 34–6, 39, 42

Index

quantification, 45, 76–82, 110, 127, 141; *see also* metrics
Quantified Self Movement, 76–7

race, 38, 48, 139, 142, 147
radicalization, 105, 149
radio, 12, 49, 67, 75, 96
Rancière, Jacques, 60
ranking systems, 79, 124, 128–9, 149
reality shows, 85, 90, 96, 100, 142
recognition theory, 6, 15, 18, 45, 46–7, 106
recommendation systems, 58
redistribution, 32
Reels, 121
refugees, 50, 108
regimes of visibility, 4, 5–7, 9–10, 52, 62, 83–106, 130, 134, 144; *see also* visibility
regulation, 58, 84–6; *see also* self-regulation
reification, 99, 101
relational labour, 13
religion, 18, 34, 64
replies *see* comments
reposts *see* shares
respect, 1, 27, 50, 145, 150; *see also* disrespect; self-respect
retweets *see* shares
Rieder, Bernhard, 128–9, 145

rights, 8, 11, 18, 22–4, 27, 134, 142, 149, 150
ritual, 66–9, 92
Rousseau, Jean-Jacques, 90

Sanghvi, Ruchi, 79
Schäfer, Mirko Tobias, 4
Schulz, Christian, 137
Scolari, Carlos A., 120
Scolere, Leah, 138, 141
search engines, 70
secondary habitus, 140
self-branding, 59, 138–9
self-confidence, 10, 20–1, 39, 59, 109, 111, 112–13, 128
self-determination, 1, 42
self-discipline, 34, 39, 92, 115
self-esteem, 2, 10, 13, 24–5, 39, 40, 59, 109, 112–13, 128, 132, 134, 148
self-expressiveness, 31, 33, 42, 91
self-identification, 16–17
self-interest, 11, 26, 27–8, 29
self-objectification, 129, 132
self-overcoming, 113, 114
self-realization, 1, 2, 20, 24, 48, 61, 98, 102, 106, 109, 112, 131, 132, 133
self-regulation, 83, 86, 93–4, 97, 134, 143, 146, 149
self-representation, 5, 7, 10–11, 30, 53, 57,

Index

85–90, 95–110, 118–19, 129, 133–4, 136, 149
self-respect, 2, 3, 10, 23–4, 39, 112–13, 128, 148
selfies, 102, 108–9, 110–11
Sena, Ercio, 50–1
sensible, distribution of the, 60, 140–1
Serelle, Marcio, 50–1
Shah, Vishal, 81
shame, 85, 88, 142
shared values, 56–7, 58
shares, 3, 7, 45, 57, 72, 74, 78, 79, 80, 109, 124, 145
short videos, 121
Shorts, 121
signals, 80, 124
Simmel, Georg, 97
slavery, 35, 50
smartphones, 15, 17, 64, 65
social capital, 120, 123–4
social class, 23, 31, 33, 37–8, 59, 85, 93, 94, 95, 112, 115–16, 142, 146
social construction, 61–2
social contract, 18–19
social esteem, 2, 24–5, 27, 72, 131, 150
social justice, 11, 33, 46, 49, 133
social movements, 2, 6, 38, 46, 54–5
social rights, 11, 23, 150
socialization, 21, 114–15, 140

sociomateriality, 147
solidarity, 20, 25, 28, 45, 115, 117, 118, 129, 132, 135, 144, 150
solidarity capital, 28
Souza, Jessé, 8, 33–43, 112–15, 117, 118, 132, 139, 140, 143, 146–7
spirit, 18, 19–20, 91
Spivak, Gayatri, 55
start-up companies, 138–9
Steinberg, Ari, 79
stereotyping, 48, 55, 57
struggle, 6, 11, 19, 20, 25, 36, 42, 52, 73–5, 96–7, 128, 132–4, 149–50
sub-citizenship, 33–4, 37, 41, 43, 146
subordinate inclusion, 115, 118, 146–7
symbolic capital, 67, 84, 110

taste, 37, 85, 112, 129, 140
Taylor, Charles, 30–7, 39, 41–2, 75, 90
technology start-ups, 138–9
television, 2, 47–8, 49–50, 51, 53, 65, 67, 75, 85, 96, 119, 133, 141–2
theatre, 50–1
theatricality, 92–3, 95, 104
Thumim, Nancy, 86, 96, 99–100, 119
TikTok, 4, 44, 75, 76, 102, 109, 121, 125
tradition, 18, 22, 24, 34–5

Index

traditional media *see* mass media
transgender people, 50–1, 147
trending topics, 67
Trilling, Lionel, 31
Turner, Graeme, 141
Twitter, 12–13, 44, 67, 74, 76, 84, 125–6, 134

unconditional recognition, 27

validation, 3, 6, 15, 59, 81, 84, 131, 132
value *see* civic value; economic value; value creation
value creation, 9, 45–6, 54, 74
Van Es, Karin, 4
Van Krieken, Robert, 93
verified accounts, 84, 123, 124–7
vertical recognition, 27
visibility
  and algorithms, 52, 89–90, 102–5, 107–8, 129, 144–5, 147
  and celebrity, 28–30, 67, 123–4, 134
  and citizenship, 10, 60, 131–2
  distribution of, 72–3
  economics of, 28–30, 74, 108, 123–4, 137
  and exclusion, 116
  figurative visibility, 73–4
invisibility, 49, 62, 73, 116, 145
  and mass media, 85, 134
  and news feeds, 73–4, 103, 129, 144–5, 147
  regimes of, 4, 5–7, 9–10, 52, 62, 83–106, 130, 134, 144
  seeking of, 5, 9, 67, 89–90, 102–5, 107–8, 122, 139, 143, 144–5
  strategies for achieving, 67, 89–90, 102–5, 107–8, 122, 144–5
  and verified accounts, 127
visibility capital, 108, 124
voice, 7, 49–51, 53, 55, 124, 126, 144–5, 147

weak recognition, 3, 130–2, 143
wearable devices, 15, 77
Weber, Brenda, 85, 142
Weber, Max, 39
welfare state, 23, 34, 36, 141
Winnicott, Donald, 21
Wolf, Gary, 76–7
Wouters, Cas, 83, 93–5, 97, 104

YouthVoice, 50
YouTube, 12, 52, 53, 56–9, 68, 76, 83–4, 88–90, 92, 99, 102–4, 121, 128–30, 137
YouTube Search & Discovery, 103–4